BARILOCHE
and the Southern Lakes

Approved by the Secretaría de Turismo y Deporte.

BARILOCHE
and the Southern Lakes
VISUAL GUIDE

ClarínX viajes

BARILOCHE
and the Southern Lakes
VISUAL GUIDE

Is a special project executed by Clarin

PRESIDENT
EDITORIAL DIRECTOR
Ernestina Herrera de Noble

PROJECT EXECUTION
Roberto Fernández Taboada
Norberto Angeletti

EDITORIAL COORDINATION
Fernando Muñoz Pace
Pablo Ravaschino

HISTORICAL ADVISER
Eliana de Arrascaeta

GENERAL EDITING
Aurelio Valdearena
Alejandra Sayago
Estela Arias

ITINERARY EDITING
Julián Chappa

PHOTOGRAPHIC SERVICES
Clarin archives
Archivo Ignacio Corbalán
Archivo General de la Nación
Roberto Rainer Cinti
Armando de Giacomo

PHOTOCHROMISM AND PRINTING
Artes Gráficas Rioplatense S.A.

First Edition. September 2001.

Argentina Visual Guides Clarín
ISBN 950-782-238-0
Bariloche and the Southern Lakes Visual Guide
ISBN 950-782-241-0

Please e-mail any comments or suggestions to **guiasturclarin@agea.com.ar,** or write to Clarin Proyectos Especiales, Tacuari 1872, Buenos Aires, Argentina. CP 1140. Customer service number: (54-11) 4510 4545.

All maps included in this book are produced in accordance with the Poder Ejecutivo Nacional, through IGM. File GG1 1997/5.

GENERAL DESIGN AND EXECUTION
Editorial Sol 90 S.L.

EDITORIAL DIRECTOR
Osvaldo Leboso

ART DIRECTOR
Fabián Cassan

PUBLISHER
Marc Llorens

ENGLISH TRANSLATOR
Michael Bunn

LAYOUT
Renata Lucena
Clara Miralles

PRODUCTION AND COORDINATION OF ILLUSTRATIONS
Andrea Giacobone

THREE-DIMENSIONAL ILLUSTRATIONS
Isidro López
Marcel Socías
Estudio de Arquitectura Tófalo-Niro

COMPUTARIZED GRAPHICS AND CARTOGRAPHY
Aldo Chiappe
Ana Gueller
Jorge Portaz

PHOTOGRAPHY
Juan Siquot

TOURIST ADVISER
Federico Kirbus

DOCUMENTALISTS
Andrea Carballo
Ramiro Espiño
Natalia Kovacic
Ricardo Marín

ARCHIVAL PHOTOGRAPHS
Mariela Petrocelli

PRODUCTION
Marta Kordon
Marisa Vivas

Our special thanks to Secretaría de Turismo y Deporte for their advice and logistical support during the creation of this guidebook.

The eastern end of Lake Huechulafquen.

Look-out point above Lake Mascardí.

Hotel Llao Llao in Bariloche.

Information kiosk.

How to Use This Guidebook

This guide is divided into three parts. GENERAL INFORMATION explains some of the history, geography and customs of Bariloche and the Southern Lakes. The ITINERARIES are our suggested routes, divided into sectors, which include maps and three-dimensional pictures of buildings and outstanding natural areas. Finally, the SERVICES section contains indispensable information for the traveler about transport, accommodation, gastronomy, leisure activities and shopping.

❶ GENERAL INFORMATION. This first part is divided into three sections: the history of the city and the region, general geography and a section on customs, concerning past and present habits. *Example on page 14.*

❷ GENERAL ITINERARIES MAP. The second part of the guide begins with a general map of all of the itineraries, and which also shows the main communication routes that connect up each of these itineraries. *Example on page 20.*

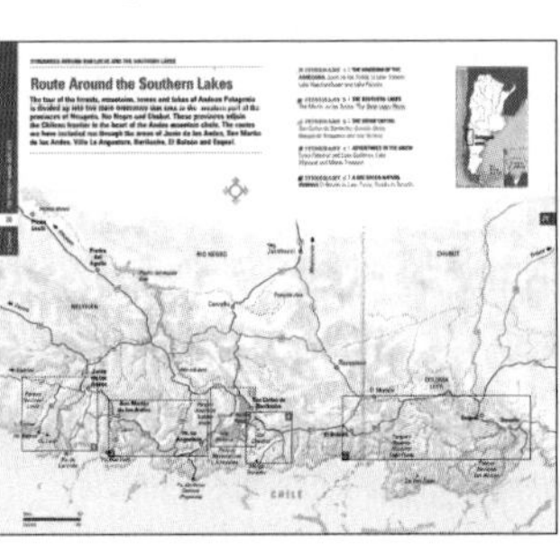

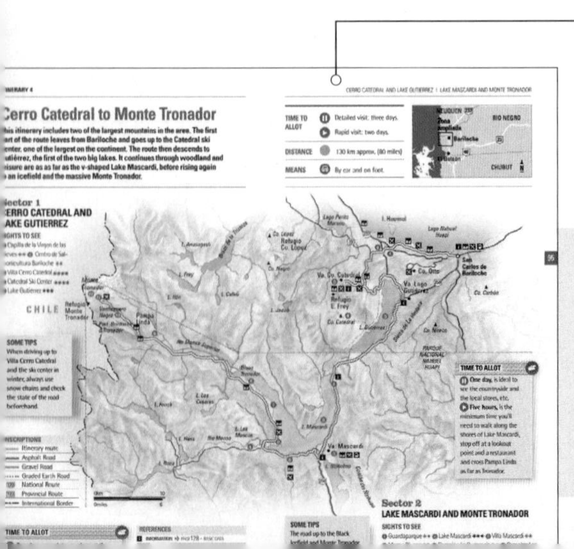

❸ THREE-DIMENSIONAL MAPS. The itinerary is divided into sectors and shown on the map. Each sector is enlarged on another detailed three-dimensional map, where the places of interest are identified by a reference number which is used in the pages that follow. *Examples on pages 66 and 94.*

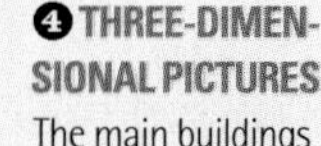

❹ THREE-DIMENSIONAL PICTURES. The main buildings and natural areas are shown in detailed three-dimensional pictures. *Examples on pages 52 and 70.*

GENERAL REFERENCES

- CONNECTION OF THE INFORMATION
- USEFUL INFORMATION
- LINK WITH OTHER PAGE
- LINK WITH A POINT OF INTEREST

SPECIAL AREAS

- HISTORICAL MONUMENT
- MANKIND PATRIMONY
- NATIONAL PARK
- BIOSPHERE RESERVE

NOTICES

- HABITS
- SPORTS
- OBSERVATORY
- FAUNA
- FLORA
- CONSIDERATIONS
- BY CAR

RANKING OF THE SIGHTS

**** Impossible to miss
*** Excellent
** Very Good
* Very Interesting

This grading system is used on the itinerary maps and sector maps.

MAPS GLOSSARY

Bay	*Bahía*	Lake	*Lago*
Beach	*Playa*	Marsh	*Estero*
Canal	*Canal*	Mesa	*Meseta*
Canyon	*Cañón*	Mount	*Monte*
Cape	*Cabo*	Mountain	*Montaña*
Cave	*Cueva*	Pampa	*Pampa*
Cliff	*Acantilado*	Peninsula	*Península*
Cove	*Caleta*	Point	*Punta*
Delta	*Delta*	Port	*Puerto*
Glacier	*Glaciar*	Ravine	*Quebrada*
Grotto	*Gruta*	Ria	*Ría*
Gulf	*Golfo*	River	*Río*
Hill	*Cerro*	Salt marsh	*Salina*
Hot springs	*Terma*	Small lake	*Laguna*
Icefield	*Ventisquero*	Straits	*Estrecho*
Inlet	*Ensenada*	Stream	*Arroyo*
Island	*Isla*	Volcano	*Volcán*
Isthmus	*Istmo*	Waterfall	*Catarata*
Jugged mountain	*Sierra*	Waterfall	*Salto*

❺ SERVICES. The third part of the guide deals with tourist services, and is comprised of the following sections: basic information, transport, accommodation, restaurants, leisure and shopping. *Example on page 142.*

LAKE VERDE

FOREST AT PUERTO BLEST

WATERFALL AT PUERTO BLEST

STREET SELLER IN EL BOLSÓN

LANDING STAGE AT PUERTO BLEST

PUMA

ARTIST'S IMPRESSION OF THE DESERT CAMPAIGN

OLD RANCH HOUSE ON VICTORIA ISLAND

INACAYAL CHIEF

OLD GENERAL STORE

RIVER ALERZAL

GENERAL INFORMATION

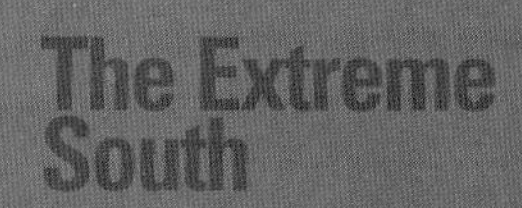

The Extreme South

As you travel south from Neuquén the Andes begins to lose height, while at the same time gaining in beauty. The old lands of the Mapuche and Pehuenches attracted the colonists, who were enchanted by the natural beauty of the region. This is the south of snowy hills, volcanoes, forests with thousand-year-old trees, wide rivers and lakes carved out by glaciers. Dotted through the landscape can be found mountain villages, existing in harmony a rich natural environment.

SUMMARY

CEFERINO NAMUNCURA

BEGONIA

MAPUCHE FABRIC

AUSTRAL PYGMY OWL

The First Settlers

Before the arrival of the Conquistadors, the area of the North Patagonia lakes was inhabited by a number of indigenous groups –hunters, fishermen and gatherers. The arrival of the horse and Spanish culture brought about significant changes in the lives and customs of these people.

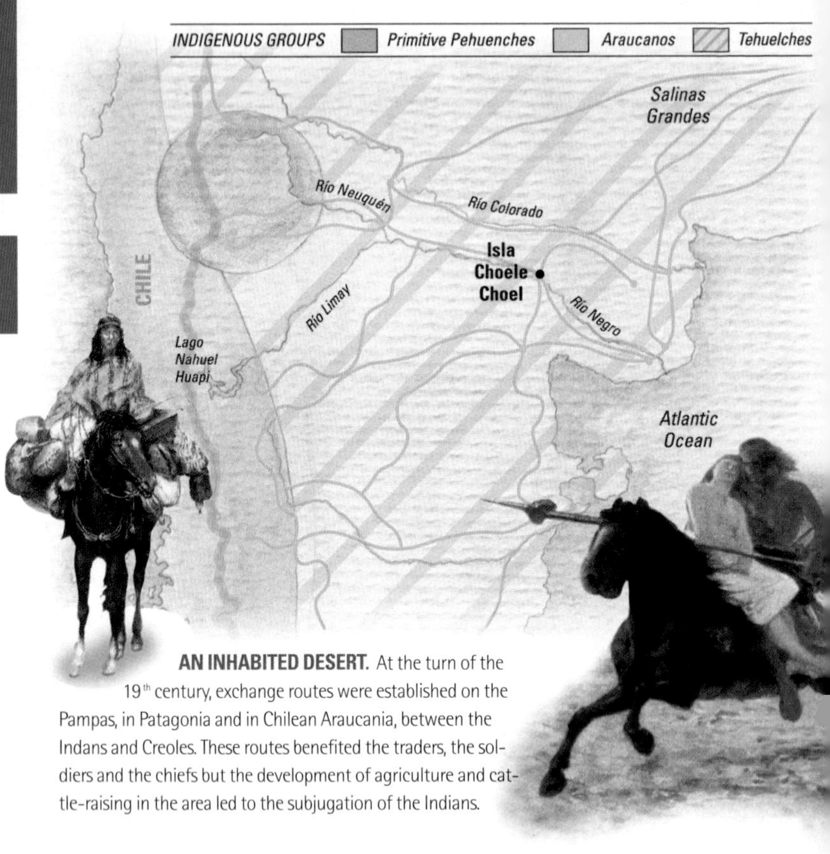

AN INHABITED DESERT. At the turn of the 19th century, exchange routes were established on the Pampas, in Patagonia and in Chilean Araucania, between the Indans and Creoles. These routes benefited the traders, the soldiers and the chiefs but the development of agriculture and cattle-raising in the area led to the subjugation of the Indians.

MAPUCHE CANOES

The area comprised of Lake Huechulafquen and Lake Lácar was the land of the Pehuenches. They traveled in dugout canoes, and the staple feature of their diet was the pine nut, the nutritious seed of the araucaria.

THE HORSE. The arrival of the horse in America changed the lives of the Indians. Horses were used as transport, for war and for food.

RELIGIOUS PIONEERS.

In the 16th century, Jesuits established missions in areas inhabited by Indians. Diego Rosales founded one in 1653, and Nicolás Mascardí set up another on Lake Nahuel Huapi.

INDIAN CRAFTS. The Indians manufactured a great many objects for use in their everyday life. At first they used clay, but later they began to use wood, metal and wool. After the Spanish conquest their designs began to imitate European styles.

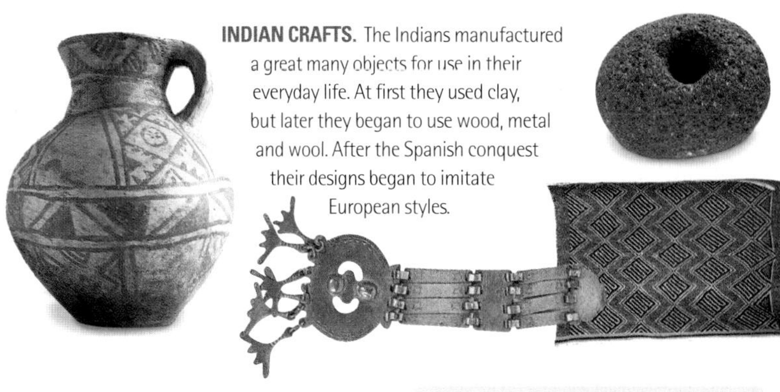

THE MAPUCHE ("Men of the earth" in their language) were the first people to inhabit the land, which they defended in battle on the arrival of the colonists. They divided up into groups, each one taking its name from the land on which they settled gave. The introduction of wire fences on the colonists' ranches in the mid-19th century robbed the Indians of their main means of subsistence: free-range cattle farming.

THE DREADED "MALONES"

"Malones" were raids carried out by different groups of indigenous people who would join together to steal animals from the Creole ranches, in order to be able to survive.

The tents in the Indian camps were made out of wood and hide, mainly taken from ponies.

LIFE IN THE INDIAN CAMPS

The Indians made their camps in areas of abundant water and pastureland. The camps were comprised of a great many tents, where they lived in large extended families. It was the center of their social, political and religious lives.

The Desert Campaign

In 1879, the government of Nicolás Avellaneda began a campaign to reassert Argentine sovereignty in Patagonia. This campaign was led by the Minister of War, Julio Argentino Roca. After five years of conflict, government forces finally managed to subdue the indigenous tribes.

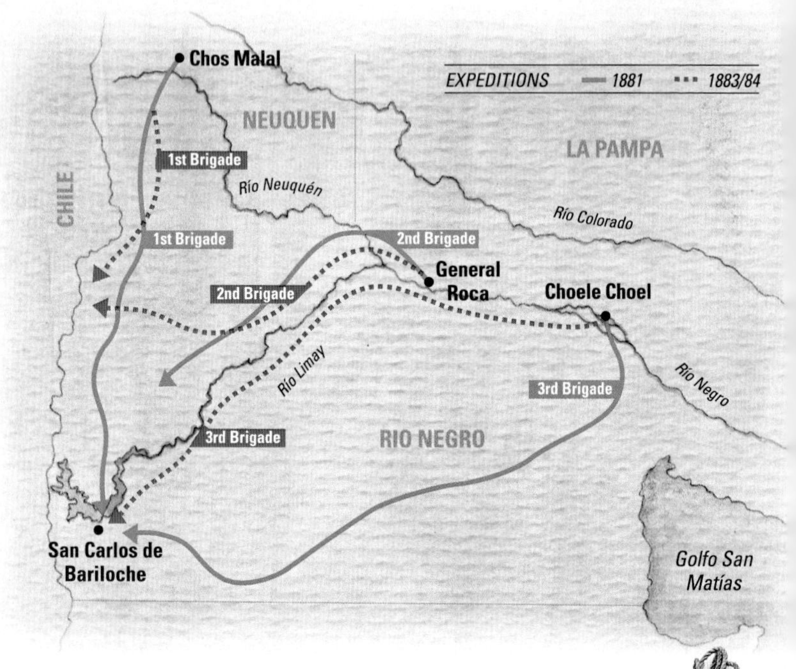

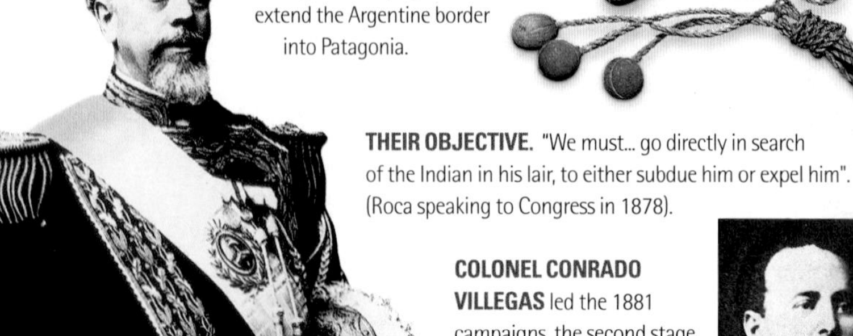

JULIO A. ROCA. In 1879, General Roca began a campaign to extend the Argentine border into Patagonia.

THEIR OBJECTIVE. "We must... go directly in search of the Indian in his lair, to either subdue him or expel him". (Roca speaking to Congress in 1878).

COLONEL CONRADO VILLEGAS led the 1881 campaigns, the second stage of Roca's plan. In that year he managed to confine the last of the Indian chiefs to Nahuel Huapi. Resistance collapsed in 1883 and 1884.

MODERN COMMUNICATIONS
Roca's troops used the telegraph, which meant they could communicate rapidly with the government in Buenos Aires.

THE LAST CHIEFS. Foyel, Cafucurá and Inacayal were among the Indian chiefs who resisted the white man's advance.

SAYHUEQUE

Valentine Sayhueque was the last Araucanian Indian chief to surrender to Roca's troops and to accept the laws and authority of the Argentine state. He was known as the chief of the "Land of Apples".

THE RELENTLESS ADVANCE

The use of Remington rifles, telegraphic communications and train transport were decisive in the victory over the indigenous people, who only had primitive weapons with which to defend themselves.

THE CAMPAIGN FORCES. General Roca's forces were comprised of **6,000** 6,000 soldiers with 7,000 horses, 1,219 mules and 270 oxen. The offensive commenced in April 1879, and within three months they had killed six Indian chiefs and 1,600 Indians.

PORTABLE TELEGRAPHS
Telegraphic networks were established during the Desert Campaign.

A Vast Green Mountain Range

The Andean-Patagonia corridor contains features which make absolutely unique: wide lakes which were the result of glacial erosion, virgin forests with thousand-year-old trees, flora and fauna exclusive to this region, permanently snow-capped mountains, volcanoes and hot springs – just some of the attractions for visitors to enjoy.

A NETWORK OF RIVERS AND LAKES

Most of Patagonia's rivers begin on the east of the Andean mountain chain and flow eastwards towards the Atlantic Ocean. In the north Patagonia lake area these rivers form a complicated network- dotted with stretches of water of glacial origin and joined up by rivers that increase in size and have progressively fewer tributaries.

L. Aluminé
L. Quillén
R. Aluminé
NEUQUEN
L. Huechulafquen
L. Lolog
L. Lácar
L. Traful
R. Limay
L. Nahuel Huapi
RIO NEGRO
L. Mascardi
CHILE
L. Escondido
L. Puelo
R. Chubut
CHUBUT
L. Futalaufquen
L. Amutui Quimei
R. Gualjaina

LAND OF MARVELS. The abundance of water in this region has led to the growth of leafy forests which, together with the mountains and lakes which were produced by glacial erosion, all go to create a landscape of great beauty.

Andean pygmy deer or Pudu.

Cóndor.

THE LAKE BASIN. This region contains 25 large lakes joined up by a network of rivers. Plant and animal life in these river systems is entirely dependent on the purity of the water.

FAUNA. The most notable mammals are the Southern Andes deer (in danger of extinction), the Pudu (only 40 cm in height) and the Puma. As for bird life, there are a great many woodpeckers in the forests, and condors in the mountains. The area is also home to a multitude of insects which feed on the wood.

Puma.

HEIGHTS AND DEPTHS. The main volcano in the Lake Region is Lanín (3, 776 meters/12,388 feet in height). This is now inactive, unlike the volcano Copahue. The area also has hot springs with therapeutic properties and abundant volcanic rocks.

3,776

DIVERSITY OF ECOSYSTEMS

The large number of valleys between the mountains, the huge lakes and high rainfall have led to the creation of different ecosystems which coexist between the Andean mountains, the rainforests and out to the Patagonia steppes.

THE HIGHEST MOUNTAINS IN THE ANDEAN PATAGONIA REGION

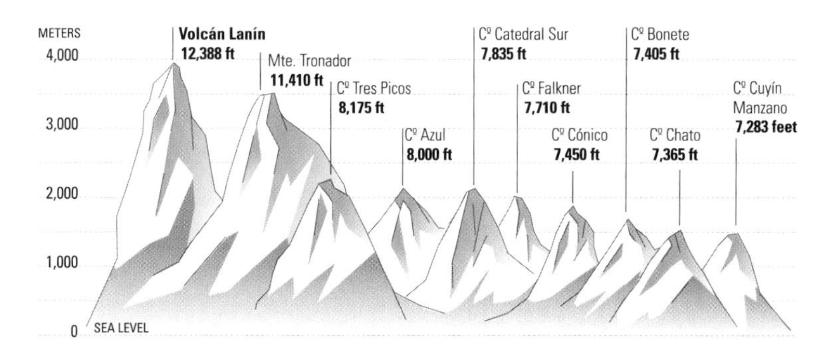

LONG-LIVING TREES

The national parks in this area contain huge old indigenous tree species such as the Chile pine, the Rauli, the cypress, the myrtle and the larch. One example is this 500-year-old coihue, which is 40 meters high, at Puerto Blest.

HOW A LAKE IS FORMED BY GLACIAL EROSION

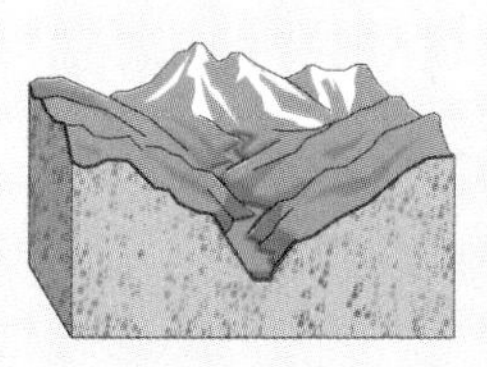

A valley before glaciation.

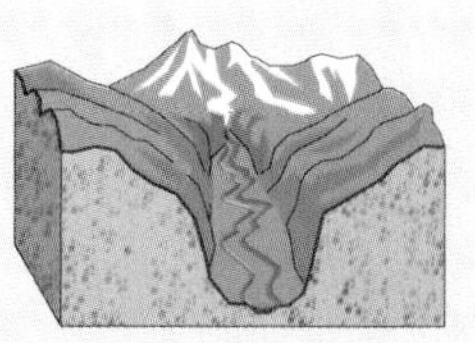

The ice digs out a U-shaped basin.

One million years ago, the area which is now the Lake Region was completely covered by glaciers. These glaciers gradually moved down through valleys that had been created by large rivers. As these huge ice masses moved forwards they gradually eroded the sides of the valley. When the glaciers receded, 11,000 years ago, the areas which had been most deeply excavated filled up with water produced by melting ice, thus creating the many lakes in the area.

Life in the Mountains and the Valleys

The Lake Region has always had an enormous influence on its inhabitants. The ways they used the natural resources and the inspiration they gained from living in such a beautiful place led to the inhabitants of this southern area creating delicious food, architecture that harmonised with the landscape, open-air sports activities and handicrafts of great quality.

CATTLE-RAISING AND FAIRS. Cattle-raising is the most important source of income in the area of Junín de los Andes. At the end of January a cattle fair is held in this area which is the most important fair of its kind in the Lake Region.

Handicrafts and local traditions

Ceramics – both Indian style and piece in the European tradition – as well as fabrics, shoes, clothes, local gastronomic specialities and carved wooden pieces are just some of the typical articles that can be found in this region. Most of these products are made using traditional methods which guarantee excellent quality.

•› MORE INFORMATION ON PAGE 142.

WOOD AND ITS MANY USES
The abundance of forests in this region means that wood is widely used for building, thus creating a particular style of integrated architecture.

PEACE AND LOVE. Places such as El Bolsón were a magnet for lot of hippies in the 1960's, who came in search of a life in harmony with nature.

ARCHITECTURE. At the turn of the 19th century, Bustillo dreamed of building "one of those picturesque mountain towns like in Switzerland and the Tyrol." The result was Bariloche and San Martín de los Andes.

THE SKIING MECCA

The region has destinations to suit all skiing tastes, from small winter ski stations such as La Hoya and Cerro Bayo to large skiing complexes of world renown, such as Chapelco and Catedral Alta Patagonia, which are among the largest to be found on the continent of South America.

•› MORE INFORMATION ON PAGE 138.

HANDICRAFT FAIRS. All of the main cities in the Andean-Patagonia region have fairs where the visitors can buy handcrafted products. The most famous one is the fair in El Bolsón.

•› MORES INFORMATION ON PAGE 142.

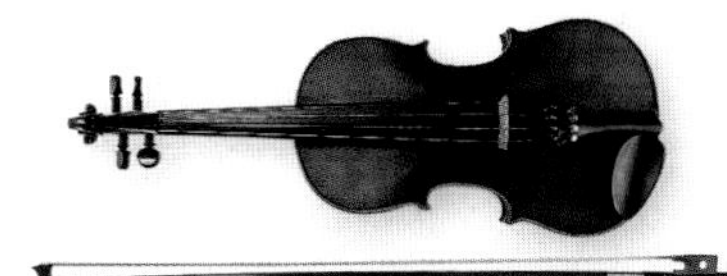

CAMPING MUSICAL. An institution dedicated to the propogation of music. The world-famous ensemble Camerata Bariloche was formed here in 1966.

Gastronomy

Tinned sweets, chocolates, smoked fish and meats are just some of the delicious food products that can be found in this region.

•› MORE INFORMATION ON PAGES 74 AND 136.

Lake fishing

The Patagonia Lake corridor contains stretches of water that are easy to reach and teeming with fish. It is a perfect region for sports fishing, as well as all kinds of other open-air sports.

•› MORE INFORMATION ON PAGES 54 AND 55

Religious tourism

One way which has recently gained in popularity of getting to know Andean Patagonia is to visit sites of religious interest. In the town of Junín de los Andes a Via Crucis of statues has been created on Cerro de la Cruz. There is also a sanctuary constructed in homage to Laura Vicuña, and a route by which visitors can find out all about her life.

•› MORE INFORMATION ON PAGE 28.

A statue from one of the stations of the Via Crucis in Junín de los Andes.

QUAY AT VILLA LA ANGOSTURA

SAN CARLOS DE BARILOCHE

THEVETIA

WOODLAND AT CERRO CHAPELCO

BARILOCHE CIVIC CENTER

BARILOCHE CATHEDRAL

HOTEL LLAO LLAO

LOG CABIN AT BOSQUE DE ARRAYANES

PARQUE NACIONAL LOS ALERCES

ITINERARIES AROUND BARILOCHE AND THE SOUTHERN LAKES

The Forest Made into Art

Between the provinces of Neuquén, Río Negro and Chubut, close to the Chilean border, Andean Patagonia becomes even more beautiful. Visitors can swim in the lakes, walk along the shores, play sports and enjoy the ski centers, or visit mountain villages, as well as prehistoric remains, protected almost-virgin forests and mountain paths. All the wonders of Argentina, with a tourist infrastructure that offers everything you could wish for.

SUMMARY

LAKE PUELO

CHAPEL OF SAN EDUARDO

CAVE PAINTINGS AT VILLA TRAFUL

ARAUCARIA

Route Around the Southern Lakes

The tour of the forests, mountains, towns and lakes of Andean Patagonia is divided up into five main itineraries that take in the western part of the provinces of Neuquén, Río Negro and Chubut. These provinces adjoin the Chilean frontier in the heart of the Andes mountain chain. The routes we have included run through the areas of Junín de los Andes, San Martín de los Andes, Villa La Angostura, Bariloche, El Bolsón and Esquel.

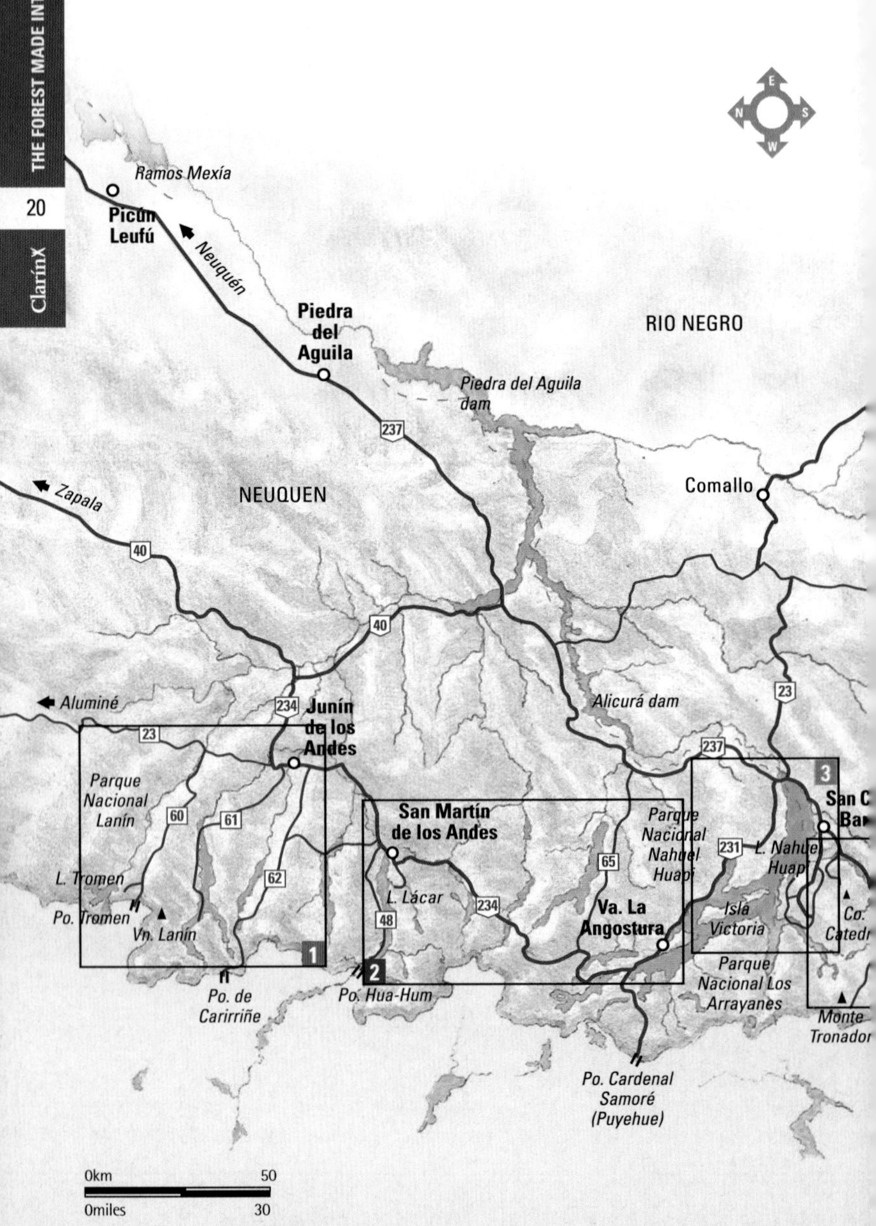

■ ITINERARY 1 | THE KINGDOM OF THE ARAUCARIA Junín de los Andes to Lake Tromen; Lake Huechulafquen and Lake Paimún.

■ ITINERARY 2 | THE SOUTHERN LAKES
San Martín de los Andes; The Siete Lagos Route.

■ ITINERARY 3 | THE SNOW CAPITAL
San Carlos de Bariloche; Circuito Chico; Bosque de Arrayanes and isla Victoria.

■ ITINERARY 4 | ADVENTURES IN THE SNOW
Cerro Catedral and Lake Gutiérrez; Lake Mascard and Monte Tronador.

■ ITINERARY 5 | A BIG GREEN NATURE RESERVE El Bolsón to Lake Puelo; Cholila to Trevelin.

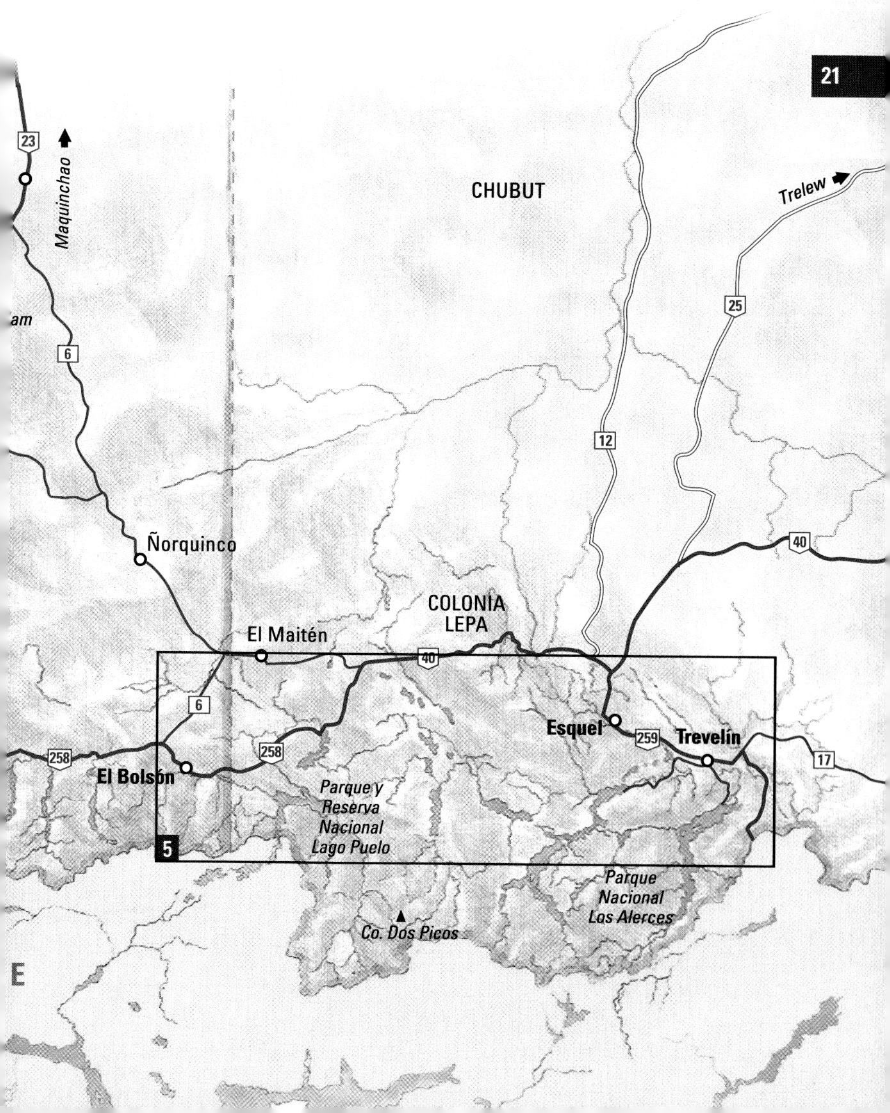

The Kingdom of the Araucaria

The area of Junín de los Andes lies in the province of Neuquén, and it still has a rich indigenous tradition. The surrounding area includes large navigable lakes, leafy woodland and the enormous Lanín volcano.

WOODLAND IN PARQUE NACIONAL LANIN

CATTLE IN CORREDOR TROMEN

WATERFALL AT CAVIAHUE

INTERIOR OF N. S. DE LAS NIEVES CHURCH IN JUNIN DE LOS ANDES

LAKE HUECHULAFQUEN

SUMMIT OF LANIN VOLCANO

ITINERARY 1

LANIN NATIONAL PARK

N.S. DE LAS NIEVES CHURCH IN JUNIN DE LOS ANDES

THE BLESSED LAURA VICUÑA

VILLA CAVIAHUE

ARAUCARIA

LAKE NORQUINCO

Lakes Tromen and Huechulafquen

The town of Junín de los Andes in the south of Neuquén province is the starting point for both of the routes included in this itinerary. The first route crosses rivers and goes through unique forests until reaching the majestic Lanín volcano, the highest point in the region. The second route runs along the banks of two great lakes, with a spectacular mountainous landscape. Both routes pass through Parque Nacional Lanín.

TIME TO ALLOT

One day, If you want to see the lakes – whether you stay on the lakeside or go sailing in a catamaran.

Five hours, If you want to walk around Lake Huechulafquen (including several stops at lookout points or a beach).

Sector 2
LAKE HUECHULAFQUEN AND LAKE PAIMUN

SIGHTS TO SEE

❶ Centro de Ecología Aplicada del Neuquén ✱✱ ❷ River Chimehuín ✱✱✱ ❸ Lake Huechulafquen ✱✱✱✱ ❹ Puerto Canoa ✱✱✱ ❺ Lake Paimún ✱✱✱

SOME TIPS

Visitors to the Huechulafquen corridor can take attractive paths such the El Bosque route. The wide range of campsites and small hotels may convince you to stay for longer than one day.

INSCRIPTIONS

- Itinerary Route
- Asphalt Road
- Gravel Road
- Graded Earth Road
- 123 National Route
- 123 Provincial Route
- International Border

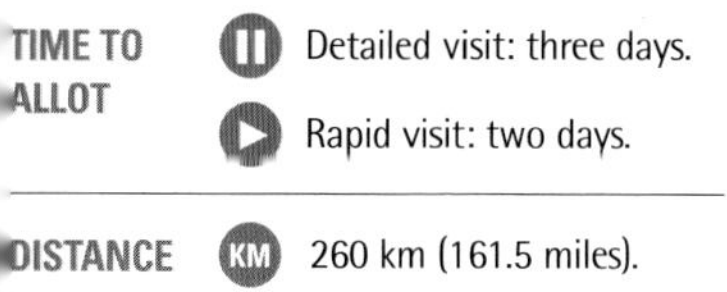

TIME TO ALLOT	Detailed visit: three days. Rapid visit: two days.
DISTANCE	260 km (161.5 miles).
MEANS	By car and boat.

Sector 1
JUNIN DE LOS ANDES TO LAKE TROMEN

SIGHTS TO SEE

❶ Junín de los Andes ✱✱✱: Iglesia Nuestra Señora de las Nieves, Museo Mapuche, Circuito Laura Vicuña. ❷ Malleo River ✱✱
❸ Parque Nacional Lanín ✱✱✱✱: Lake Tromen, Resguardo Aduanero Tromen, Lanín volcano, Paso Internacional Mamuil Malal.

SOME TIPS

Do not try any of the paths that go up Lanín volcano without first checking with the Park Warden on the state of the paths and the weather forecast.

TIME TO ALLOT

Two days, one day to look around Junín de los Andes and another to explore the corridor.

In one day you can walk out of Junín de los Andes up to the international path, where you can enjoy a beautiful view of Lanín, and then get back before nightfall.

REFERENCES

- INFORMATION •› PAG.128 - BASIC DATA
- SERVICE STATION •› PAG.130 - TRANSPORTATION
- AIRPORT •› PAG.131 - TRANSPORTATION
- HOTEL •› PAG.132 - ACCOMODATION
- RESTAURANT •› PAG.136 - RESTAURANTS

Junín de los Andes to Lake Tromen

This route begins at the city of Junín de los Andes, on the banks of the River Chimehuín, which is very popular with fishermen and still has traces of Mapuche indian culture. Take a one-day trip and go fishing or swimming in River Malleo or Lake Tromen, wander through araucaria forests or skirt the edge of the incredible Lanín volcano.

❸ PARQUE NACIONAL LANIN ✱✱✱✱

Places of interest:

- Lake Tromen
- Resguardo Aduanero Tromen
- Lanín volcano
- Paso Internacional Mamuil Malal

Fishing at Lake Tromen *(Parque Nacional Lanín).*

L. Tromen
❸
Sierra de Mamuil Malal
CHILE
Volcan Lanin

The area of the Resguardo Aduanero Tromen is the starting point for a number of footpaths *(Parque Nacional Lanín)*.

Climbers can scale Lanín volcano *(Parque Nacional Lanín)* 3,776 m (12,388 ft) in height by a number of different routes.

0km 10
0miles 6

SIGHTS TO SEE

- **IGLESIA NUESTRA SEÑORA DE LAS NIEVES**
- **RIVER MALLEO**
- **LAKE TROMEN**
- **LANIN VOLCANO**

FACTS

8,000 KILOMETERS OF EVANGELIZING
Domingo Milanesio (1843–1922), a local priest, traveled 8,000 km (over 5,000 miles) on evangelical missions.

INSCRIPTIONS

- Asphalt Road
- Gravel Road
- Graded Earth Road
- 123 National Route
- 123 Provincial Route
- International Border

❷ RIVER MALLEO ✱✱

The River Malleo begins near the Chilean border at one end of Lake Tromen and finishes when it meets the River Aluminé. The river is ideal for salmon fishing.

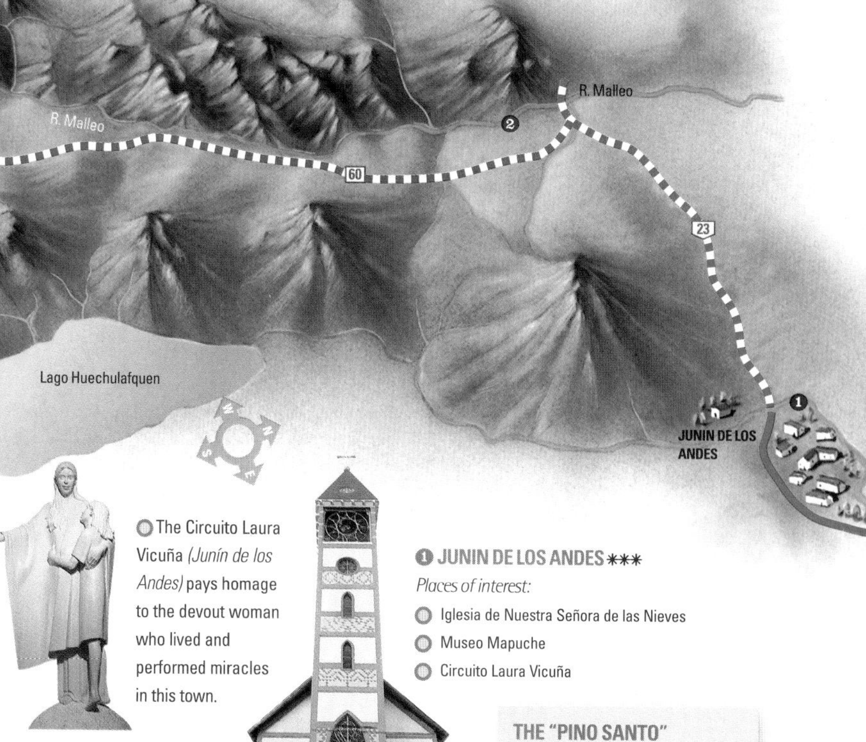

◎ The Circuito Laura Vicuña *(Junín de los Andes)* pays homage to the devout woman who lived and performed miracles in this town.

◎ The Church of Nuestra Señora de las Nieves *(Junín de los Andes)* includes features from local Indian culture.

❶ JUNIN DE LOS ANDES ✱✱✱

Places of interest:

- ◎ Iglesia de Nuestra Señora de las Nieves
- ◎ Museo Mapuche
- ◎ Circuito Laura Vicuña

THE "PINO SANTO"
This is the name of the famous araucaria on RP 80 which once sheltered a family caught in a snowstorm.

This route begins in Junín de los Andes, located in a valley on the banks of the River Chimehuín.

JUNIN DE LOS ANDES 1

This was the first city founded in Neuquén province, and was built on the fortress of Junín de los Andes, founded in 1883. Though it lacks the size or tourist infrastructure of other tourist centers in the region, Junín de los Andes is a great starting point for a number of easy, pleasant walking routes through areas of Indian cultural heritage.

IGLESIA DE NUESTRA SEÑORA DE LAS NIEVES ①

Church. This Church was officially opened in 1959, and has been recently remodeled using a number of Mapuche-inspired motifs which are combined with the original Neo-Gothic architecture. The most striking feature is the tower with its colored dome, which is visible from every point in the town. The atrium contains a statue and as a religious relic of the Blessed Laura Vicuña, while the Church interior includes vaulting with lancet arches decorated with shapes inspired by local nature, such as the Chile pine leaf.

MUSEO MAPUCHE ②

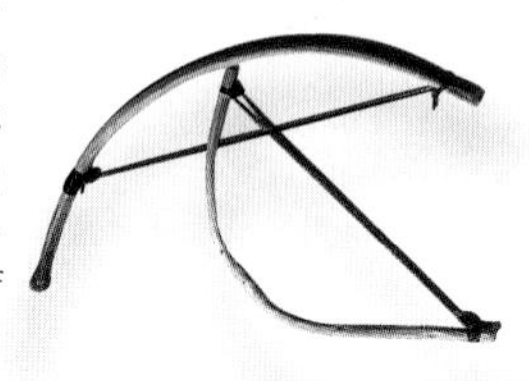

Mapuche musical instrument, used in ceremonies.

The Mapuche Museum. Tis museum was opened in 1988 with the aim of preserving and exhibiting the culture of the region's original inhabitants. The museum is built on land ceded by the city's religious bodies. Visitors can see objects from the Mapuche culture that have been found at archeological sites such as Covunco Abajo cave in Chile. Pieces include everyday objects (charm collars, containers and carved wooden spoons), fossil remains and wind and percussion instruments such as the trutruca (the sacred Mapuche drum), the pillolai and the p'füllka.

||| OPEN: MONDAY, WEDNESDAY AND FRIDAY FROM 5 PM. TRIPS TO THE MUSEUM ARRANGED IN THE TOURIST OFFICE: TEL. (02944) 49-1160.

THE RIVERSIDE PATH

Situated on the right of Junín de los Andes, the 50 km (31.7 miles) of Chimehuín riverside path is used all year as a recreation area and for fishing – especially for salmon.

CIRCUITO LAURA VICUÑA ③

Laura Vicuña in the Virgin's arms.

The Laura Vicuña Route. The Chilean Laura Vicuña (1891-1904) was beatified after sacrificing her life for her mother. Her life in Junín de los Andes is commemorated by a route showing the house where she died, the hermitage in which she suffered her illness, the site of the old school where she lived (now the Church of N. S. de las Nieves) and the Fosbery ranch. The Tourist Office will provide you with details of the route.

▶ *Leave Junín de los Andes on RN 234 towards Zapala till the RP 23 junction. A road leads to the River Malleo bridge, after 22 km (13.5 miles).*

VIA CRUCIS

In 2003, a Via Crucis was built on Cerro de la Cruz, west of Junín. The monument combined Christian and Mapuche elements and as a 40-meter-long figure of Christ coming out of the ground. Plus two bas-reliefs and fourteen stations telling the history of Junín and of Laura Vicuña.

THE ARAUCARIA, A SACRED TREE

In Neuquén province there are lots of Chile pine (araucaria or pehuén) forests, especially on the path to Lake Tromen.

Some of these extraordinary trees live as long as 1,000 years. They have very hard leaves, rough bark 10-15 cm thick, and they grow to a maximum height of 40m (131 feet). They produce pine cones, each of which contain some 200 pine nuts. The high nutritional value of the Chile pine nut makes it an ideal food, and in fact it was the staple diet of the Mapuche people.

RIVER MALLEO 2

This river interweaves with the path until its end. The River Malleo, which is ideal for fishing, flows through a typical Patagonia steppe landscape featuring Chile pine woods as well as mixed woodland that includes exotic species such as the Pine. The River Malleo begins at Lake Tromen, almost on the Chilean border, and finishes when it meets the River Aluminé, beyond the RP 23.

▸ *Fork left onto the RP 60, a flat gravel road. A few minutes later, turn right towards the Mapuche town of Atreuco. You'll now have a wonderful view of the mountains. 10 km (6.2 miles) further on, turn right to the Mapuche reserve of Chiquilihuin. At the 45 km (27.9 miles) mark on the RP 60, you reach the park.*

PARQUE NACIONAL LANIN 3

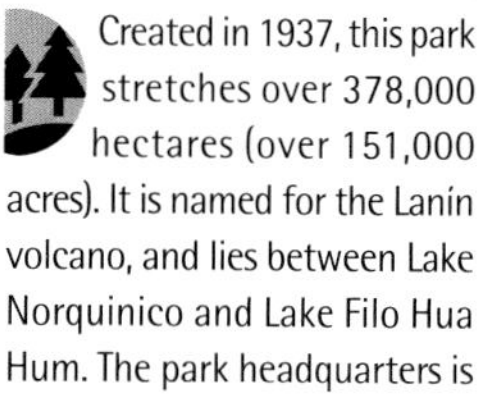

Created in 1937, this park stretches over 378,000 hectares (over 151,000 acres). It is named for the Lanín volcano, and lies between Lake Norquinico and Lake Filo Hua Hum. The park headquarters is located in San Marttín de los Andes. This is a park of importance since it contains woodland species not found in another protected areas, such as the Chile pine, the Pellín oak and the Raulí. As for the park's fauna, Red Deer were introduced in 1922, and the species has been a great attraction for hunters since 1946. Trout have also been introduced.

▸ *A Chile pine forest leads to the Frontier Guard post. North of this, there is a 3 km-long path (1.8 miles) that leads to Lake Tromen.*

LAKE TROMEN 

Beach on the banks of Lake Tromen.

To the north of Lanín lies Lake Tromen, from which the River Malleo flows at its southeast point. The waters is clear or greenish in color, and there is a heavy swell. The beaches are of volcanic sand. On the lakeside is the inn Refugio del Lago Tromen, very popular with fishermen.

Araucarias (Chile pine trees) with the Lanín volcano silhouetted in the background.

All walks around Lanín volcano start at the Tromen Frontier Guard post, which also provides information for walkers.

RESGUARDO ADUANERO TROMEN ②

Tromen Frontier Guard Post. This is a National Police post, as well as being the Customs control and the park warden's office. It is also the starting point for a number of paths that lead to Lake Tromen (see previous subsection) and Lanín volcano. Visitors wishing to climb to the top of the volcano should notify the park warden, who will advise them on the equipment they will need.

Behind the Police post there is a track for vehicles which runs through a Lenga forest as far as the foot of the volcano.

The Lanín volcano presides over the wild landscape of the eponymous park.

LANIN VOLCANO

This volcano, at 3,776 m (12,388 feet) in height, is effectively the highest mountain in the national park that bears its name. It was first climbed in 1897 by Rodolfo Hauthal. Its topography made it an important crossing point on Andes, since the Spanish conquest until today. The Argentine side has a shallow gradient, while on the Chilean side, following the course of the River Trancura, it is virtually flat until it reaches the Pacific. During the 18th century this was the crossing point for the Mapuche, who would take cattle from the southern part of Buenos Aires province to sell them in Chile. This trade declined after the construction of military forts in the 19th century.

MORE INFORMATION ON PAGES 32-33.

Beyond the customs office building, the RP 60 continues until the Chilean border, along the Mamuil Malal International Pass.

PASO INTERNACIONAL MAMUIL MALAL ④

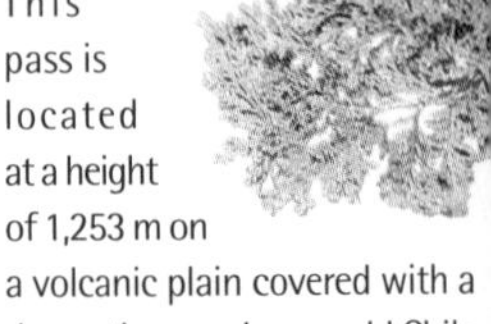

This pass is located at a height of 1,253 m on a volcanic plain covered with a dense, thousand-year-old Chile pine forest. The path marks the dividing line between Lanín national park, on Argentine land, and Villarica which stands on Chilean soil. Looking from clearings in the forest, visitors have a marvelous view of the majestic snow-capped Lanín volcano. ■

THE LEGEND OF LANIN VOLCANO

A local folktale tells the story of how years ago the god Pillán, who lived on the volcano's, became very angry because some young men from the Huanquimil tribe killed some deer.

The tribe's witch doctor said that to pacify the god they would have to sacrifice Huilefún, the chief's beautiful daughter. So, the bravest young man in the tribe carried Huilefún up onto the volcano, but when he reached the top, a condor grabbed the girl and tossed her into the crater, thus silencing the volcano forever.

The Good Waters

To the north of Junín de los Andes lies Neuquén province, which contains two very beautiful routes: the Pehuenia path, which runs past lakes, and the Copahue/Caviahue provincial Park, with volcanoes and health-giving hot springs.

◀ THE PEHUENIA ROUTE This includes Aluminé, Villa Pehuenia and some beautiful lakes (Norquinico, Quillén, Pulmarí and Rucachoroi, among others) surrounded by colorful vegetation and lots of waterfalls.

▶ COPAHUE HOT SPRINGS 2,500 m (8,202 feet) above sea level, are great for alleviating aches and pains, owing to their high sulfur content.

▼ ARAUCARIA FORESTS The sacred tree of the Mapuche can be found in great numbers .

◀ COPAHUE VOLCANO The sacred tree of the Mapuche can be found in great numbers on both routes.

▼ LA CASCADA ESCONDIDA this "Hidden waterfall" stands in Copahue/Caviahue provincial park. The water falls 15 m (49 feet) , amidst vegetation that includes Ñires (a type of beech), Chile pines and Mutisia, an indigenous species of climbing shrub.

Copahue/Caviahue Provincial Park: 80 km (49.7 miles) from Junín de los Andes on the RN 40 and the RP 21. Aluminé is 120 km (74.5 miles) north of Junin de los Andes on the RP 23.

Lanín Volcano

The summit of this volcano – 3,776 m (12,388 feet) – is permanently snowcapped, and is clearly visible from many different points in Lanín national park. Lanín is popular with mountaineers, while non-climbers can enjoy wonderful footpaths that skirt the volcano. Climbers may make use of the fully-equipped refuge shelters.

THE VOLCANO Lanín is permanently covered with snow. The last time it showed any volcanic activity was in the 18th century, and it has not rumbled since 1918. When they erupt, snow-capped volcanoes can unleash a torrent of water, mud and ash.

ICE. *There are five glaciers in the Lanín area. One of them is on the north side, while the others are on the west and the south sides.*

LENGAS, *Ñires and Chile pines are the main components of the mixed woodland at the foot of the volcano. A little further south you can ind the Coigue, the Raulí and the Pellín oak.*

THE ARAUCARIA or Chile pine is a major feature in the Lanín landscape; the soil produced by volcanic rock is perfect for this species. Grows at over 800 m above sea level.

CRYSTAL-CLEAR WATER *abounds in the 11 lake basins that can be found in the park, with all their lakes, lagoons, rivers and streams.*

USEFUL INFORMATION

ADDRESS: RP 60 (without number).

VISITS: Before entering the volcano area, always seek information at Lanín national park headquarters, in the park warden's office or at the park radio. station: (02972) 42 -7210 and 42 -7204. Also, please register at the park warden's office at Puerto Canoa and Rio Turbio.

FACTS

INSECT-PROOF

The thick bark of the Chile pine, which grows all around Lanín volcano, secretes a resin which keeps away insects.

SMOKESTACKS. The volcanoes Lanín, Quetrupillán, Villarica, Choshuenco, an d Achen make up the "Pacific ring of fire".

EMERGENCY SHELTERS *can be found on the volcano, equipped with emergency food supplies.*

GOING UP. There are a number of routes up Lanín, classified into three groups: trekking, mountain chain and high mountain. To get to the top you need to be in good physical condition, but always notify the park warden in advance and take the necessary equipment.

EQUIPMENT. *You will need suitable clothes, food and medication to climb Lanín. The park wardens will give you an equipment list..*

ALWAYS CHECK. *The weather forecast and the state of the paths before you climb.*

The Neuquén Dinosaurs

The province of Neuquén is one of the most important places in the world for paleontologists. Many fossil remains of dinosaurs have been discovered here in recent years, some of which are of great scientific importance. Millions of years ago, the Neuquén basin was home to a multitude of dinosaurs.

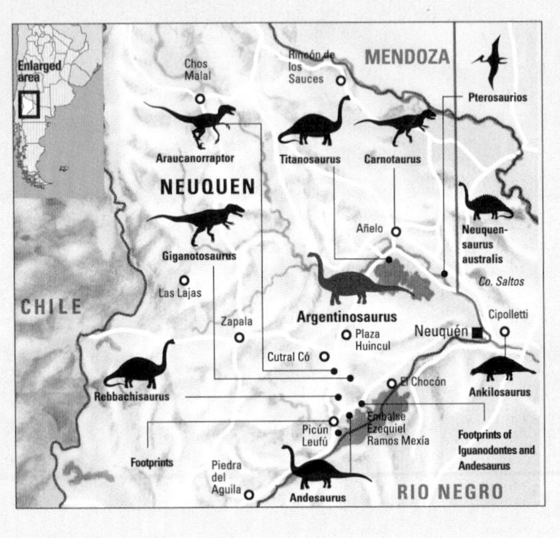

◄ LAND OF GIANTS Approximately 95 million years ago, before the Andesrose from the ground, the central desert of Neuquén province was a fertile area of enormous plants and many different species of dinosaurs.

GIGANOTOSAURUS
Giganotosaurus carolinii
Length: **16 m (52 ft)**
Weight: **8 tons**
Lived: **95 million years ago**
Site found: **El Chocón**

▼ THE GIGANOTOSAURUS almost 16 m long, was the largest carnivorous dinosaur in the world. In spite of its enormous size, it possessed excellent balance when running, turning and coming to a halt.

▼ MOLDS, such as this Giganotosaurus skull have been put together as part of a reconstruction process.

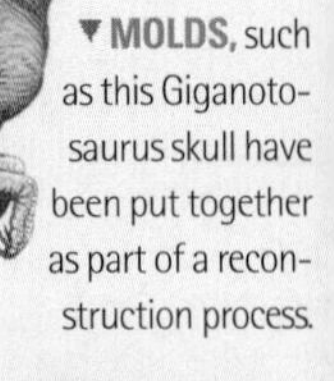

The Discoverers

▼ The paleontologist Rodolf Coria (curator of the Plaza Huincul Museum), Rubén Carolini and other specialists found a great many fossil remains.

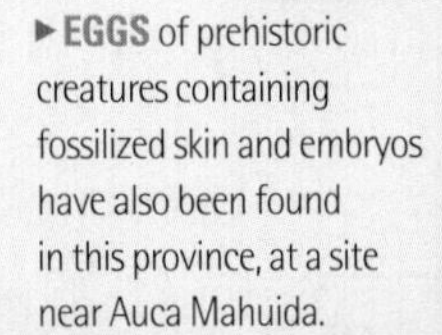

► EGGS of prehistoric creatures containing fossilized skin and embryos have also been found in this province, at a site near Auca Mahuida.

HOW FOSSILS ARE EXCAVATED

Excavating fossil remains is a long process. Once the layers covering the fossil has been removed, all fissures are sealed and work continues using bradawls and paint brushes. Before fossils are removed , they are covered with tissue paper and plaster.

▶ **FLORENTINO AMEGHINO,** the father of paleontology in Argentina, carried out 175 scientific studies between 1875 and 1911, classifying fossils such as the Gliptodontus *(photo).*

Excavations

▶ Over thirty sites containing fossil remains have been discovered in Neuquén province during the last 30 years. The sedimentation process that took place on this land helps to conserve the fossils, and the University of Comahue continues to receive reports of new finds.

◀ **THE ARGENTINOSAURUS,** was an enormous herbivorous dinosaur from the Neuquén area. Its remains (including vertebra, a femur and other bones) were discovered in 1987. Experts believe that it was the largest dinosaur in the world.

ARGENTINOSAURUS
Argentinosaurus huinculensis
Weight: **100 tons**
Length: **40m (131 feet)**
Lived: **95 million years ago**
Site found: **Plaza Huincul**

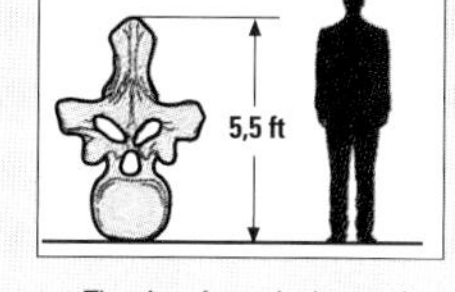

The size of one single vertebra 1.65 m (5.4 feet)

ONE ARGENTINOSAURUS *weighed as much as sixteen elephants..*

FIGURE OF A MAN TO SCALE

Lake Huechulafquen and Lake Paimún

This route begins at Junín de los Andes and follows the course of the River Chimehuín until it reaches Huechulafquen, a huge crystalline lake where you can go out on a catamaran or visit the lakeside forests and beaches. This lake area is considered to be a paradise for fishing enthusiasts.

❺ LAKE PAIMUN ✱✱✱

This lake is joined to Huechulafquen by a narrow stretch of water, close to which both lakes also join up with Lake Epulafquen.

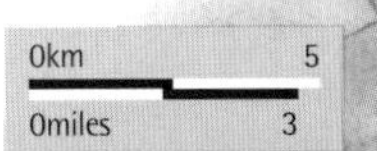

Lago Tromen
Volcán Lanín
Lago Paimún
❺
❹
COMUNIDAD MAPUCHE CAÑICUL
Lago Epulafquen
Lago Curruhué Grande

TO THE HOT SPRINGS

Although they are nearby, the hot springs by Lake Epulafquen cannot be reached from this sector - visitors can only get there from the Curruhué corridor (see page 38).

❹ PUERTO CANOA ✱✱✱

The José Julián *sails from this point, off through the lakes. There is also a small hotel and a quincho (outside barbecue area).*

INSCRIPTIONS

▬	Asphalt road
═	Gravel road
·······	Graded Earth Road
123	National Route
123	Provincial Route

TIME TO ALLOT	Detailed visit: four days.
	Rapid visit: three days.
DISTANCE	About 260 km (161 miles).
MEANS	By car and boat.

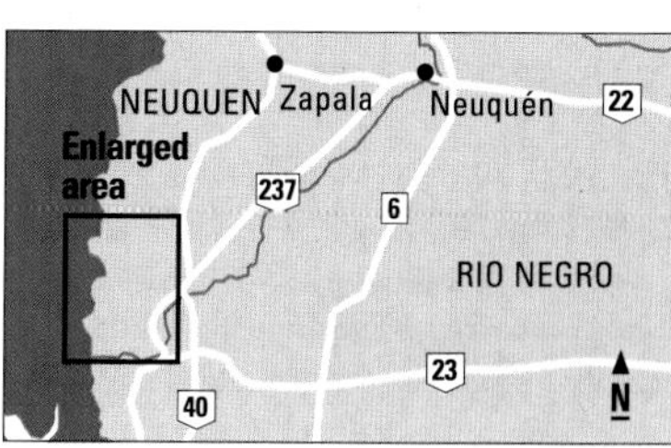

Sector 2
THE SIETE LAGOS ROUTE

SIGHTS TO SEE

❶ Lake Meliquina ✱✱ ❷ Lake Machónico ✱✱✱ ❸ Valle del lago Hermoso ✱✱✱ ❹ Vullignanco waterfall ✱✱✱ ❺ Lake Villarino and Lake Falkner ✱✱✱ ❻ Lake Traful ✱✱✱ ❼ Villa Traful ✱✱✱✱ ❽ Lake Espejo ✱✱✱ ❾ Boca del Correntoso ✱✱✱ ❿ Villa La Angostura ✱✱✱✱

TIME TO ALLOT

One day, is enough for this route, with occasional stops.
Five hours, is enough to complete the whole route while stopping off at a few lookout points without taking the turnoff to Villa Traful.

SOME TIPS

The numerous campsites and small hotels along the route, plus the beautiful walks in Villa Traful and Villa La Angostura, make it a place that deserves a longer stay.

REFERENCES

INFORMATION ➜ PAGE 128 - BASIC DATA
AIRPORT ➜ PAGE 131 - TRANSPORTATION
SERVICE STATION ➜ PAGE 130 - TRANSPORTATION
HOTEL ➜ PAGE 132 - ACCOMODATION
RESTAURANT ➜ PAGE 136 - RESTAURANTS

San Martín de los Andes

Located in a valley between mountains on the banks of Lake Lácar, the city of San Martín de los Andes is the epicenter of this route. Apart from the old town, unmissable sights include the beaches and leisure areas of Lake Lácar, the lookout points and Chapelco winter sports center.

❷ LAKE LACAR ✱✱✱✱

Ferries sail from the quay at San Martín de los Andes, heading for lovely beaches and many other nooks and crannies, traveling almost as far as the Chilean border.

❸ MIRADOR DE LAS BANDURRIAS ✱✱

This lookout point, which is near San Martín de los Andes, gives a great view of the city and the lake.

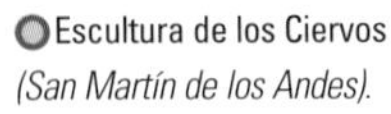

Escultura de los Ciervos *(San Martín de los Andes).*

48
Lago Lácar ❷
QUILA QUINA ❺
Catritre ❹
Arroyo Grande
234

❹ PLAYA CATRITRE ✱✱✱

On the Avenida San Martín *(San Martín de los Andes)* there are lots of stores built in the mountain style.

❶ SAN MARTIN DE LOS ANDES ✱✱✱✱

Places of interest:

- Avenida San Martín
- Plaza San Martín
- Municipalidad
- Museo Primeros Pobladores
- Intendencia P. N. Lanín
- Escultura de los Ciervos
- Quay

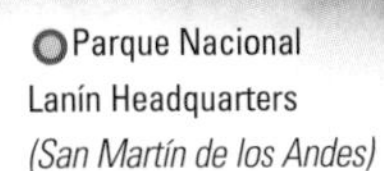

Parque Nacional Lanín Headquarters *(San Martín de los Andes)*

SIGHTS TO SEE

- SAN MARTIN DE LOS ANDES
- LAKE LACAR
- QUILA QUINA
- CERRO CHAPELCO

FACTS

COLONIAL MEADOWS
Vega del Maipú (up the valley, east of San Martín) was one of the first colonial estates.

INSCRIPTIONS

- Asphalt Road
- Gravel Road
- Graded Earth Road
- 123 National Route
- 123 Provincial Route

5 QUILA QUINA ★★★
Lakeside chalets and a beach with all services make this a perfect spot for a visit.

0km 5
0miles 3

VEGA DEL MAIPU
SAN MARTIN DE LOS ANDES
Rio Calbuco
234
19
6
7
Cerro Chapelco

AUTUMN COLORS
In autumn, the San Martín de los Andes woodland is a gorgeous sight – a kaleidoscope of reds, ochres and yellows.

7 CERRO CHAPELCO ★★★★
Visit this lookout point by taking a path trough a wood.

Statue in Plaza San Martín *(San Martín de los Andes).*

6 MIRADOR ARRAYAN ★★
Visit this lookout point by taking a path through a wood. Also has a restaurant and teahouse.

40 km (24.8 miles) south of Junín de los Andes on the RN 234 (and 150 km/93 miles north of Bariloche on the RN 237 and the RP 63), is the town of San Martín de los Andes, by Lake Lácar. This is the starting point for itinerary 2.

SAN MARTIN DE LOS ANDES 1

Night view of San Martín de los Andes.

Situated in a valley which is bordered on its west side by Lake Lácar, San Martín de los Andes is one of the finest tourist centers in all Andean Patagonia. The marvelous location (which shelters its 20,000 inhabitants from Andean winds) is highlighted by the mountain-style wood and tile-roofed buildings. It is also a well-planned city with an excellent hotel infrastructure (established in the 1970s) and a wide selection of excursions and leisure alternatives available in the surrounding areas, the most important of these being the Chapelco ski station.

► *The tour of San Martín de los Andes starts on the city's main drag, Avenida San Martín, and goes from the traffic circle at the crossing with Calle Curruhinca to Lake Lácar.*

Craft shops in Avenida San Martín

AVENIDA SAN MARTIN ①

From one end to the other (where it ends at the lake), this 13-block street includes the city's two main squares (Plaza Sarmiento and Plaza San Martin), as well as most of the hotels, restaurants, stores and shopping malls (featuring handicrafts, fabrics, chocolates and teahouses), banks, airline companies and several public buildings.

► *Three blocks from the traffic circle stands Plaza Sarmiento, while two blocks further on, behind Capitán Drury, lies Plaza San Martín.*

PLAZA SAN MARTIN 

S. Martín Square. In the middle of this square green plaza there is a statue of General San Martin on horseback. The square is location for the city's main institutions, such as the Lanín National park Headquarters, the City Council, the Municipal Tourist Board, the First Settlers Museum and the post office. There are also several handicraft shops nearby.

Statue in Plaza San Martin.

► *On one side of the square, at the corner with General Roca, a tall stone tower rises above the City Council building.*

MUNICIPALIDAD 

City Council. The main institution in the city is crowned by a rectangular stone tower with a clock at the top. The gray of the tower combines with the white of the façade in Plaza San Martin and the red of the doors, windows, balconies and roof.
III ROSAS AND GENERAL ROCA.

The houses of San Martín de los Andes, with Lake Lácar to the left.

Lanín National Park Headquarters is made out of logs, stone and slate.

► *Near the City Council is a small wooden building – the First Settlers Museum.*

MUSEO PRIMEROS POBLADORES ④

First Settlers Museum. This small museum tells the history of the first inhabitants of San Martín de los Andes and surrounding areas, with several different displays. Visitors can see archeological remains, documents and photos from the period when it was founded (1898) as well as objects from the early days of skiing.

III INFORMATION: TEL. (02972) 42-7347.

► *On the opposite side of the square to the Museum and the City Council stands Lanín National Park Headquarters.*

PARQUE NACIONAL LANÍN HEADQUARTERS ⑤

This building, which was inaugurated in 1946, has the same design features as other national park headquarters in the area (i.e. the Nahuel Huapi park headquarters in San Carlos de Bariloche). This typically mountain-style building, made of logs and slate tiles, is surrounded by lovely gardens containing indigenous species from the park.

III LANÍN NATIONAL PARK HEADQUARTERS: EMILIO FREY 749. TEL. (02972) 42-7233.

► *Walk along Avenida San Martin towards the lake; you'll see the Deer Sculpture when you get to the lakeside road.*

ESCULTURA DE LOS CIERVOS ⑥

The deer, the emblem of the city

The Deer Monument. The Red Deer was introduced into the region and is now the emblem of San Martín de los Andes. Another deer sculpture stands in front of the City Council.

► *Avenida San Martin ends at the quay. Beautiful view of the lake.*

THE QUAY 

On the Avenida Costanera M.A. lakeside road there is a quay where visitors can take a boat tour of Lake Lácar to nearby beaches, or off to the western end, which is almost in Chile.

Quay by the waters of Lake Lácar.

► *There is a beautiful panoramic view of the winding Lake Lácar from the entire length of the lakeside path (called Costanera) and from the quay.*

LAKE LACAR 2

This post-glacial lake is 26 km (61 miles) long, 2 km (1.2 miles) wide and has a maximum depth of 275m (902 feet). Entering from the north, Lácar is the first lake in Argentina which flows out into the Pacific ocean.

It includes some popular beaches and recreational areas such as Quila Quina. ⊙

Lake Lácar, seen from one of the many lookout points in the area.

Starting from Lake Lácar, cross the bridge over the Pocahullo River and a 900 m (0.5 miles) path leads up to Bandurrias lookout point. Or get there on the RP 48, taking the left turnoff after 2 km (1.2 miles). Bandurrias is 5 km (3 miles) further up.

MIRADOR DE LAS BANDURRIAS | 3

Lookout point. This point gives you a view of virtually all of Lake Lácar, part of San Martín de los Andes and Villa Quina Quina - looking to the south, east and west. You can also see the mountains Chapelco (and the ski center) and Abanico.

Lookout point above Lake Lácar.

► Take the southbound RN 234 (asphalted) out of San Martín de los Andes and after 4 km (2.4 miles) take the turnoff on the right to Playa Catritre.

OFF TO LAKE LOLOG

Another recommended trip: take the northbound RP 62 out of San Martín de los Andes to the Lolog lakes (see photo left), Curruhué Grande and Curruhué Chico, the Epulafquen hot springs and the Chilean border – a 90-km (55.9 miles) stretch of swampland, forests and lakeside campsites.

PLAYA CATRITRE | 4

Catritre Beach. This beach on Lake Lácar is located almost directly opposite Bandurrias lookout point. Playa Catritre is a sandy, slightly sloping beach. There is a bar, a restaurant and a campsite which has all the necessary services for campers.

CERRO ABANICO

Near to San Martín de los Andes stands Cerro Abanico, a mountain 1,100 m high. It is an old volcano which split into two, after which one half collapsed into Lake Lácar.

Swimming at Playa Catritre.

► A couple of kilometers further on along RN 234, take another turnoff to the left. The RN 108 (gravel surface) goes through a Pellín oak forest and after 12 km (7.4 miles) reaches Quila Quina.

QUILA QUINA | 5

Visitors can reach Quila Quina by two different routes: by car (see above) or by boat. Villa Quila Quina was created in 1945 as part of the program devised by Exequiel Bustillo (the head of the national parks) for Lanín national park. It includes chalets by a sandy beach, while nearby there is the Arroyo Grande waterfall and a number of hot springs.

Jetty at Quila Quina on Lake Lácar.

There is a marvelous view of Lake Lácar from the Arrayan lookout point.

▸ *Take a trip out to hotel Sol de los Andes – only 2.5 km (1.5 miles) from San Martín de los Andes on the RP19 (asphalt surface). From here, 500 m of road leads to a right turn which goes to a lookout point.*

MIRADOR ARRAYAN | 6

Lookout point. The road up to the lookout point over Lake Lácar goes through woodland with broom and cypress trees, which becomes denser towards the top. The lookout point has a panoramic view of the city of San Martín de los Andes and Lake Lácar. There is also a tea-house and a restaurant offering cakes, confectionery and typical local dishes.

▸ *Take the Siete Lagos RN 234 out of San Martín de los Andes and after 15 km (9.3 miles) of asphalt road you reach a crossroads. Turn left onto the RP 19, which goes up to Chapelco.*

CERRO CHAPELCO | 7

Chapelco ski station, created in the 1970s, is one of the finest in the country. It has 140 hectares of skiable surface ranged between 1,200 m (3,936 feet) and 2,000 m (6,561 feet) above sea level. Visitors can use the slopes, or go Alpine or cross-country skiing, snowboarding, mountain walking, hang-gliding and sledging. The central complex is comprised of 900 m² (0.5 sq. miles) of cafes, bars, restaurants and leisure services. ■

•› INFORMATION ON PAGES 52-53

Skiers at Chapelco ski station.

MAP OF THE SLOPES AT CHAPELCO SKI STATION

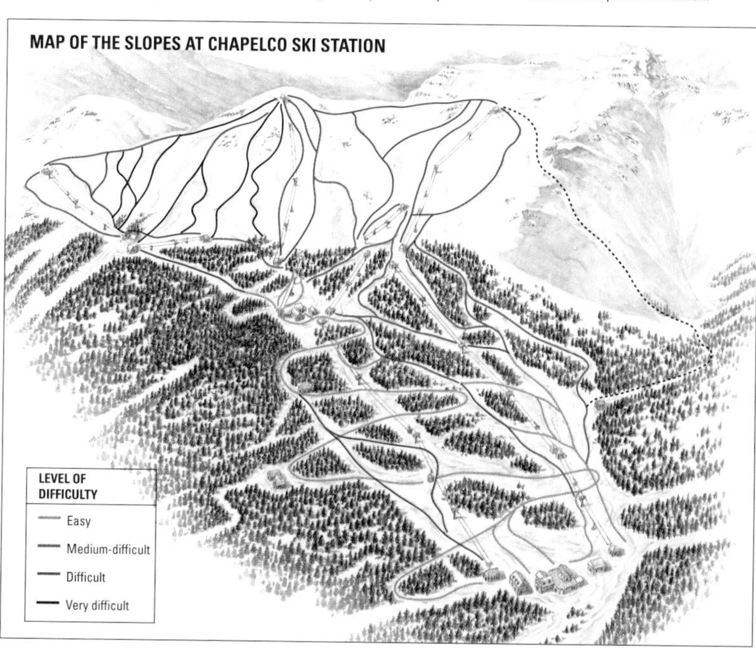

Cerro Chapelco

The main ski station in Neuquén province is close to San Martín de los Andes. In addition to its privileged location, Chapelco offers a variety of ski slopes for all levels, a wide range of high quality services in the station and on the slopes, and is manned by an attentive and highly qualified staff.

THE GONDOLA LIFT *transports skiers to the top of the slopes in 7 minutes and 45 seconds.*

RESTAURANTS and high quality cafes are located at the base of the station and on the midway platforms. Mountain food, fondues, chocola te drinks and cakes are just some of the specialties available.

SNOWBOARDING *in the snowboard park near the "El Palito" lift visitors can enjoy the four specialties of this sport (half-pipe, parallel slalom, big air and fun park).*

THE WINTER SEASON in Chapelco begins in mid-June and ends around the end of September. The snow on the ski slopes is powder, packed powder and spring snow.

THE CHAPELCO SKI SCHOOL, one of the most prestigious in Argentina, was opened in 1974. Today, as many as one hundred ski instructors give classes to between 5,000 and 6,000 people each season, and even teach abroad.

USEFUL INFORMATION

ADDRESS: RP 19 s/n. Tel. (02972) 42-7845.

VISITS: The Chapelco Ski Center, located 19 km (12 mi) from San Martín de los Andes, has hotels, hostels and cabins in the station at the base of the lifts. A wide range of day and multi-day tickets are available for ski-lifts, equipment rental, and ski lessons with discounts for families.

ANDEAN BOBSLEDDING

In summer a giant slide is installed on the ski slopes. Visitors fly down its broad curves on alpine sleds.

CAPACITY. *The station's lifts can carry 12,000 skiers per hour. Visitors enjoy its 140 hectares of skiable terrain. The longest uninterrupted descent is some 5,300 meters long (17.400 feet).*

CHAPELCO AVENTURA. This is the name of the station in summer, when the offering includes trekking, children's playground, trails, archery, mountain swimming pool, riding 4 x 4's and other options.

DOGSLED TRIPS *pulled by huskies through snowy forests is a recently added attraction of this station.*

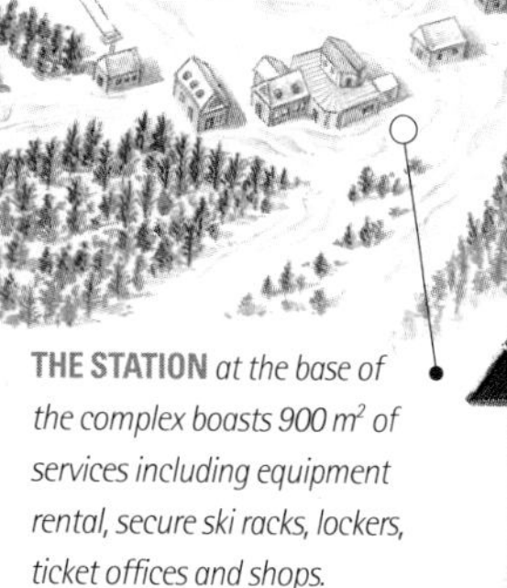

THE STATION *at the base of the complex boasts 900 m² of services including equipment rental, secure ski racks, lockers, ticket offices and shops.*

Fishing in the Lakes Region

The profusion of large lakes and rivers makes the Andean Patagonia a paradise for fishing lovers. The superb conditions in the area have attracted fishermen from all over the world, who come in search of the excellent salmonids that abound here.

SEASON. The fishing season begins in November and closes in April. Exact dates vary and can be found in the fishing regulations.

Lures

▸ Three types of artificial lures are mainly used for fishing in the lakes and rivers of the south: the fly or imitation of an insect; lures that emulate a small fish; and spoons, which work like lures.

◂ **THE MALLEO RIVER**, near Junín de los Andes, is one of the most popular rivers in Argentina among foreign fishing enthusiasts. In it one can find many hiding holes of the brown trout.

▾ **CHIMEHUIN.** in the province of Neuquén, the River Chimehuin well known for its famous mouth is famed as the place where record catches of brown trout occur in Argentina.

Near Junín de los Andes and the Lanín Volcano, the Chimehuin River is a superb fishing area.

INSECT LIFE AND FISHING
Fly tiers have to spend long hours observing the movements of insects in order to imitate, using artificial means, the flight and movement of the species which the various types of fish feed on.

Types of Fishing

▶ **FLY FISHING** requires specific skills for the preparation and casting of the fly.

◀ **SPINNING** is fishing with lures from a coast or beach.

▼ **SPECIES.** The most important in terms of both quantity and quality are the landlocked salmon *(left)*, the brown trout *(center)* and the rainbow trout *(right)*.

Large salmonids are abundant in Andean Patagonia.

Gear

Depending on the place and the species, fishing tackle varies according to size and weight. A heavier reel is used for trolling *(photo left)*, and lighter gear is used for fly fishing *(photo right)* to give the fish a chance.

▶ **CLOTHING.** Clothing used by fishermen in the southern lakes includes: Polaroid sunglasses, pants, hat and vest. The vest replaces the tackle box, since fishermen cover long distances.

The Siete Lagos Route

Going south from San Martín de los Andes on the RN 234, this itinerary winds its way past several beautiful glacial lakes along the border between the Lanín and Nahuel Huapi National Parks. If its lookout points and beaches were not enough, the mountain villages of Villa Traful and Villa La Angostura stand out because of their impeccable surroundings.

❽ LAKE ESPEJO ✱✱✱

has crystalline waters and two bays. Lake Espejo Chico is nearby.

❸ VALLE DEL LAGO HERMOSO ✱✱✱

❾ BOCA DEL CORRENTOSO ✱✱✱

In this spot, the narrow Correntoso River, only 300 m long (1,000 feet), connects the waters of Lake Correntoso to those of Lake Nahuel Huapi.

L. Espejo
0km 10
0miles 6
234
L. Correntoso
L. Nahuel Huapi
VILLA LA ANGOSTURA
L. Traful
65
VILLA TRAFUL

❿ VILLA LA ANGOSTURA ✱✱✱✱

One of the loveliest villages in the area.

❼ VILLA TRAFUL ✱✱✱✱

Situated on the banks of Lake Traful, this small village is much frequented by fishermen and offers the visitor abundant and excellent excursions in the vicinity.

SIGHTS TO SEE

- LAKES VILLARINO AND FALKNER
- LAKE TRAFUL
- VILLA TRAFUL
- VILLA LA ANGOSTURA

FACTS

ARROYO PARTIDO

On the Pilpil Pass there is a curious external watershed or divide: a single water course splits and runs to both the Atlantic and the Pacific.

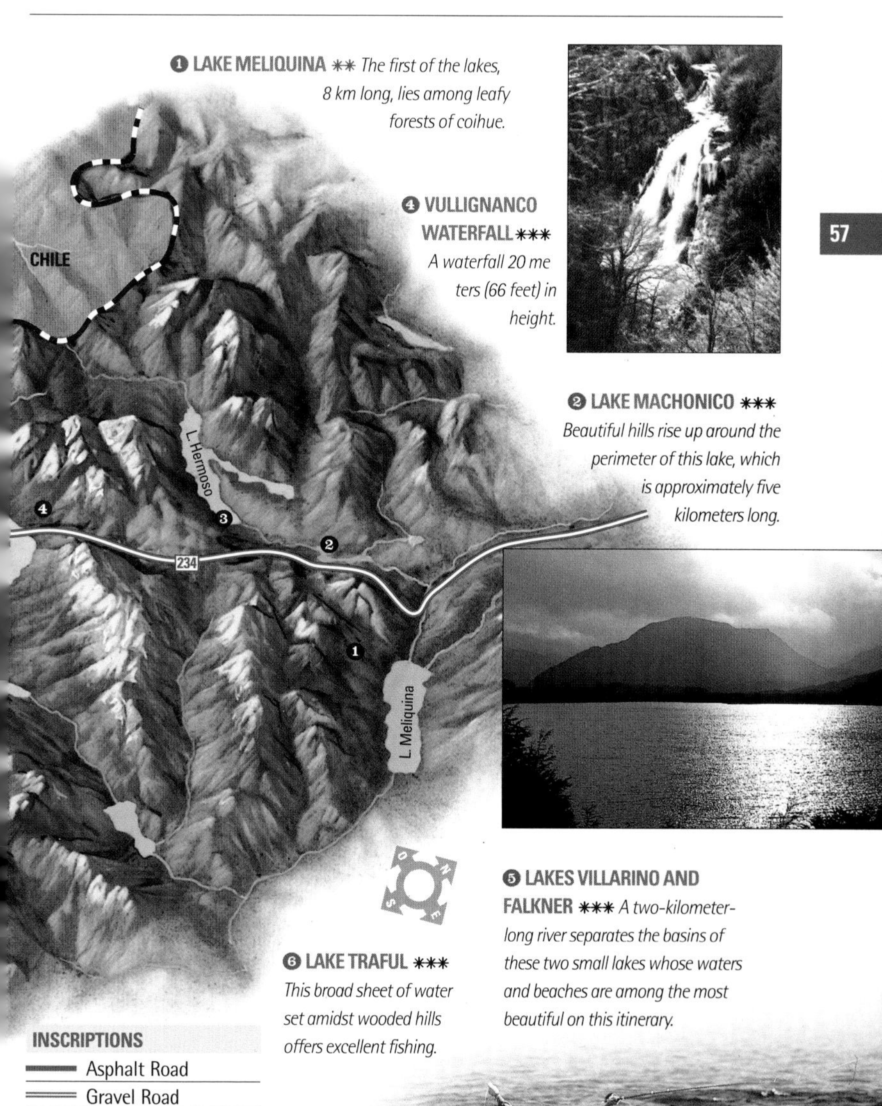

❶ LAKE MELIQUINA ✱✱ *The first of the lakes, 8 km long, lies among leafy forests of coihue.*

❹ VULLIGNANCO WATERFALL ✱✱✱ *A waterfall 20 meters (66 feet) in height.*

❷ LAKE MACHONICO ✱✱✱ *Beautiful hills rise up around the perimeter of this lake, which is approximately five kilometers long.*

❺ LAKES VILLARINO AND FALKNER ✱✱✱ *A two-kilometer-long river separates the basins of these two small lakes whose waters and beaches are among the most beautiful on this itinerary.*

❻ LAKE TRAFUL ✱✱✱ *This broad sheet of water set amidst wooded hills offers excellent fishing.*

INSCRIPTIONS

- Asphalt Road
- Gravel Road
- Graded Earth Road
- 123 National Route
- 123 Provincial Route
- International Border

Leave San Martín de los Andes by RN 234 going south. After 10 km you pass the turnoff to Cerro Chapelco, and shortly you come to the divide of the Arroyo Partido river, which drains towards both the Atlantic and the Pacific. Around kilometer 25 there is a turnoff left for Meliquina.

After the Lake Machónico lookout point, the road enters the Lake Hermoso valley.

LAKE MELIQUINA 1

Along the eight-kilometer shoreline you will find camping areas and several cabins set in coigue forests. Continuing along the west shore you will eventually connect one hundred kilometers further on with RN 237 passing Confluencia, which is on the Big Circular Route.

► *After the Meliquina turnoff, RN 234 continues to the south. Vehicles climb a grade as the road runs along the shores of Lake Machónico, which has a viewpoint on the shore.*

LAKE MACHONICO 2

Approximately five kilometers long (more than 5 miles long), Lake Machónico has wooded shores with small hills along the shoreline. The vegetation of the area comprises forests and other more steppe-like areas. In fall the leaves on the trees turn ochre and red, creating an impressive landscape.

► *Soon after the viewpoint overlooking Lake Machónico, the road enters the Lake Hermoso valley. A turnoff leads down to the lake.*

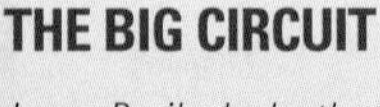

VALLE DEL LAGO HERMOSO 3

This valley, colonized in the nineteen forties, formerly included a big game hunting territory. There is a wilderness campground above the Hermoso River, and a bar on the road. The lake is not visible from the road, and can be reached after 2.5 kilometers.

► *6 km further on, the RN 234 runs from the Lanín National Park to Nahuel Huapi National Park. The Vullignanco waterfall is on the right side of the road 5 km further on (around 3 miles).*

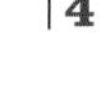

VULLIGNANCO WATERFALL 4

View of the Vullignanco waterfall.

The waters of this impressive waterfall pour down 20 meters (65 feet) into the Filuco river. The waterfall can be seen from a look out point where there is also a parking area.

► *Return to the RN 234, now running through the Nahuel Huapi National Park. Shortly afterwards you will see Lake Falkner on the left, separated from Lake Villarino by just 1.5 km (1 mile).*

THE BIG CIRCUIT

Leave Bariloche by the RN 237 along Limay River. Pass El Anfiteatro and El Valle Encantado (amazing rock formations, such as El Dedo de Díos (the Finger of God) and Los Dos Vascos (the Two Basques). At Confluencia the route goes to Villa Traful, Villa La Angostura and Bariloche.

SNOW CONDITIONS
To travel along the Seven Lakes Itinerary without problems it is well to remember that winter snowfall can close the road to vehicular traffic. In warm and temperate seasons the route is open.

LAKES VILLARINO AND FALKNER | 5

Since they lie close together, separated only by a narrow isthmus where the Villarino River passes, we describe these two lakes together. After passing a bridge, you can see a fisherman's hostel on the left, owned by the mother of the plastic artist Marta Minujin. A slight slope leads up to the Villarino viewpoint, which offers excellent views of the area.

INTERESTING SPOTS IN VILLA TRAFUL

Travelers can enjoy many highly recommended walks and excursions in the vicinity of Villa Traful.

The Cerro Lemu waterfall (66 feet) is nineteen kilometers distant and surrounded by woods populated by birds. The Bosque Sumergido (Underwater Forest) and the Gruta de la Virgen attract divers and are located in one of the cliffs overlooking the lake. The Lagunas Mellizas (twin lagoons), the Vigilante Hill, the Arroyo Cataratas waterfall and the trails leading to Lake Filo Hua Hum are other points of interest.

► *2 km (1.2 miles) further on lies Lake Escondido, the smallest lake on the circuit, with an unusual greenish color. Some 6 km later (3.7 miles) lies the Pichi Traful Park Ranger Station. 2 km further on the left are the bays of lake Traful.*

LAKE TRAFUL | 6

The mouth of the Pichi Traful river at the north end of the lake of the same name is a excellent spot for fly fishing and camping. Lake Traful is a large body of water with a surface area of 80 square kilometers (31 sq. miles) set in the Andes mountains, with beaches and spectacular forests surrounding it. .

Lake Traful, a mirror of water inside the Nahuel Huapi National Park.

► *The route continues to the south following the course of the Traful River until it reaches a turnoff to the left. Leave RN 234 to take this turnoff, which runs along the southern shore of Lake Traful for 30 kilometers (18.6 miles) until it reaches Villa Traful.*

VILLA TRAFUL | 7

This small mountain village of just 300 inhabitants is frequented by fishermen owing to the excellent fishing in Lake Traful. Points of interest include its dock and the dreamlike landscape that can be see from its restaurants, cafes and houses built on the surrounding hillsides. Hotels, hostels, cabins as well as campsites with and without facilities offer accommodation, and there are many possibilities for interesting excursions.

Take the road in the opposite direction back to the RN 234. Turn left at the junction. After 2.5 km (2 miles) you will pass the Quintupuray hostel, famous for its delicious cakes. The road runs alongside Lake Correntoso, passing by a turnoff to Lake Espejo Chico (where there is a campsite). Two kilometers along the road there is a turnoff on the right leading to Lake Espejo.

Wharves in Villa La Angostura, on the waters of Lake Nahuel Huapi.

LAKE ESPEJO 8

Viewpoint above Lake Espejo.

In the area around Lake Espejo (Lake Mirror) there is a complex beside a beach with accommodation, all services and a campsite. This other sheet of water is closer to the Chilean border, which can be reached near the southernmost point of the lake.

Take RN 234 around the lake until you reach the left turn that connects with RN 231, which arrives shortly at the mouth of the Correntoso.

BOCA DEL RIO CORRENTOSO 9

Mouth of the Correntoso River. This is last point from which Lake Correntoso can be seen, the point where its waters flow into Lake Nahuel Huapi by way of the Correntoso River. A hotel opened in 1922 occupies a spectacular site on the mouth of the river.

Shores of Lake Correntoso.

Continue along RN 231, which follows the shores of the enormous Lake Nahuel Huapi, the largest in the region. After a few kilometers the first buildings of the town of Villa La Angostura appears on the right side of the road.

VILLA LA ANGOSTURA 10

Located in a valley between the Belvedere, Inacayal and Bayo hills, and washed by Lake Nahuel Huapi, this beautiful mountain village was first settled in 1934. Its natural beauty is complemented by its sloping roofs, its wharves, parks, woods and viewpoints. Numerous bungalows, cabins, hostels, cafes and convenience stores were built with views of the lake, and the Bayo ski station operates at the base of the hill of the same name.

THE MINIMO RIVER

From the high bridge over the Correntoso River on the isthmus separating Lake Correntoso from Lake Nahuel Huapi, you can see the scant 300 meter (1,000 feet) total length of the river, which makes it one of the shortest rivers in the world.

The Colors of the Andes

The cold temperate forests of Andean Patagonia favors the development of a vast native flora, as surprising and substantial in its large scale (immense centuries-old trees) as in the multitude of flowers which add, if possible, even more color to the landscape.

▲ **LUPINS,** irises, foxgloves and other flowers surprise us with their unbelievable shapes and colors, which reveal all their splendor in spring and summer.

► **EL CHILCO,** la mutisia, hippeastrum and other flowers are native to this region.

◄ **SHRUBS** and plants which are endemic in the country are common. This *costilla de vaca* which grows in the Lago Puelo National Park is just one example.

◄ **THE FORESTS** include decid ous and evergreen trees that reach up to 60 meters (200 feet) in height, such as the coigue.

► **THE DIAMETER** of some trees in the region, such as the larch, increases only one millimeter each year.

► **FUNGI** such as the Llao Llao grow on the branches of trees and on damp ground.

▲ **SHAPES** and colors unknown in other parts of the world are displayed by the myrtle tree and the araucaria.

The Snow Capital

San Carlos de Bariloche and its environs is one of the major tourist destinations in the coun-try. Its secret is that it is a mountain city, featuring the large Lake Nahuel Huapi, a forest uniqu in the world and a large and high quality range of hotels and leisure opportunities.

BOSQUE DE ARRAYANES

THE CATHEDRAL OF NUESTRA SEÑORA DE NAUEL HUAPI

SUNSET OVER LAKE NAHUEL HUAPI

JETTY IN PUERTO QUETRIHUÉ

PANORAMIC VIEW OF LAKE NAHUEL HUAPI

CENTRO CIVICO IN BARILOCHE

PUERTO SAN CARLOS IN BARILOCHE

ITINERARY 3

HOUSE IN BARILOCHE

SAN EDUARDO CHAPEL

VICTORIA ISLAND

PISTOL ON DISPLAY IN THE MUSEO DE LA PATAGONIA

FOREST LANDSCAPE

HOTEL LLAO LLAO

Bariloche and Circuito Chico

San Carlos de Bariloche is situated on the shores of the large Lake Nahuel Huapi, the most important city in Andean Patagonia, and one of the largest tourist destinations in Argentina. The first part of this itinerary is through the city, built in the style of a European mountain village. The Circuito Chico Route, which begins in Bariloche, is a drive that features an abundant and luxurious range of accommodation. A third sector of the route takes you by catamaran to the extraordinary Bosque de Arrayanes.

Sector 3
BOSQUE DE ARRAYANES AND ISLA VICTORIA

SIGHTS TO SEE

❶ Puerto Pañuelo ✻✻ ❷ Bosque de Arrayanes ✻✻✻✻ ❸ Isla Victoria ✻✻✻✻ Sendero Playa del Toro, Sendero Cerro Bella Vista, Sendero de las Sequoias.

TIME TO ALLOT

A full day, is required to take this organized excursion. The schedule depends on the timetable of the catamaran that makes the trip to Arrayanes and Victoria Island.

SOME TIPS. The Bosque de Arrayanes (myrtle forest) in the Quetrihué peninsula can be visited by crossing the lake from Puerto Pañuelo, or else by taking the trail that starts from the neighboring town of Villa La Angostura to the north.

Sector 2
CIRCUITO CHICO

SIGHTS TO SEE

❶ Parque Ecoturístico Cerro Viejo ❷ Chocolates Fenoglio ❸ Club Náutico ❹ Velas y Cerámica Belén ❺ Teleférico Cerro Otto ❻ Isla Huemul ✻ ❼ Cerro Campanario ❽ Ahumadero Familia Weiss ❾ Casa de Muñecas ❿ Capilla de San Eduardo ⓫ Hotel Llao Llao ⓬ Bahía López ✻✻✻✻ ⓭ Colonia Suiza ⓮ Cervecería Blest.

TIME TO ALLOT

A full day, is the best option to visit the Small Circular Route in detail.

In a half-day, you could complete the Route, stopping only at the most notable points.

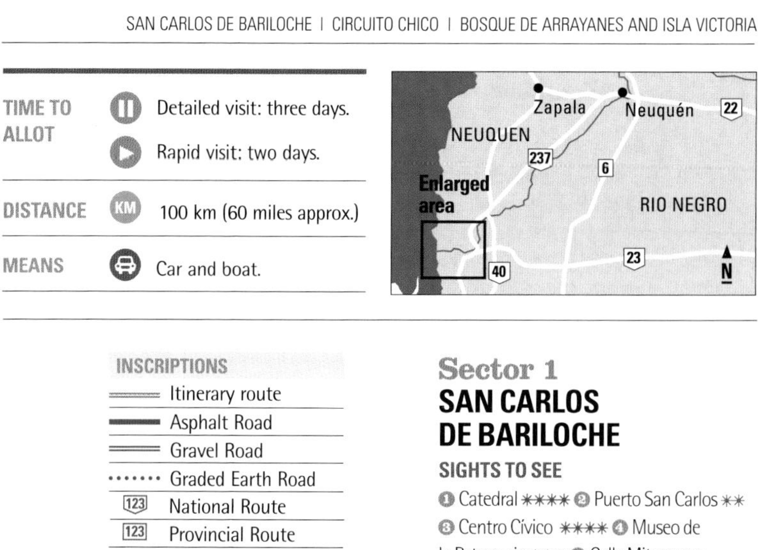

TIME TO ALLOT	Ⅱ	Detailed visit: three days.
	▶	Rapid visit: two days.
DISTANCE	KM	100 km (60 miles approx.)
MEANS	🚗	Car and boat.

INSCRIPTIONS

- Itinerary route
- Asphalt Road
- Gravel Road
- Graded Earth Road
- 123 National Route
- 123 Provincial Route
- International Border

Sector 1
SAN CARLOS DE BARILOCHE

SIGHTS TO SEE

❶ Catedral ✱✱✱✱ ❷ Puerto San Carlos ✱✱ ❸ Centro Cívico ✱✱✱✱ ❹ Museo de la Patagonia ✱✱✱ ❺ Calle Mitre ✱✱✱ ❻ Capilla de la Inmaculada ✱✱✱ ❼ Paseo de las Colectividades ✱✱ ❽ Paseo de los Artesanos ✱✱ ❾ Intendencia P.N. Nahuel Huapi ✱✱✱ ❿ Club Andino Bariloche ✱✱

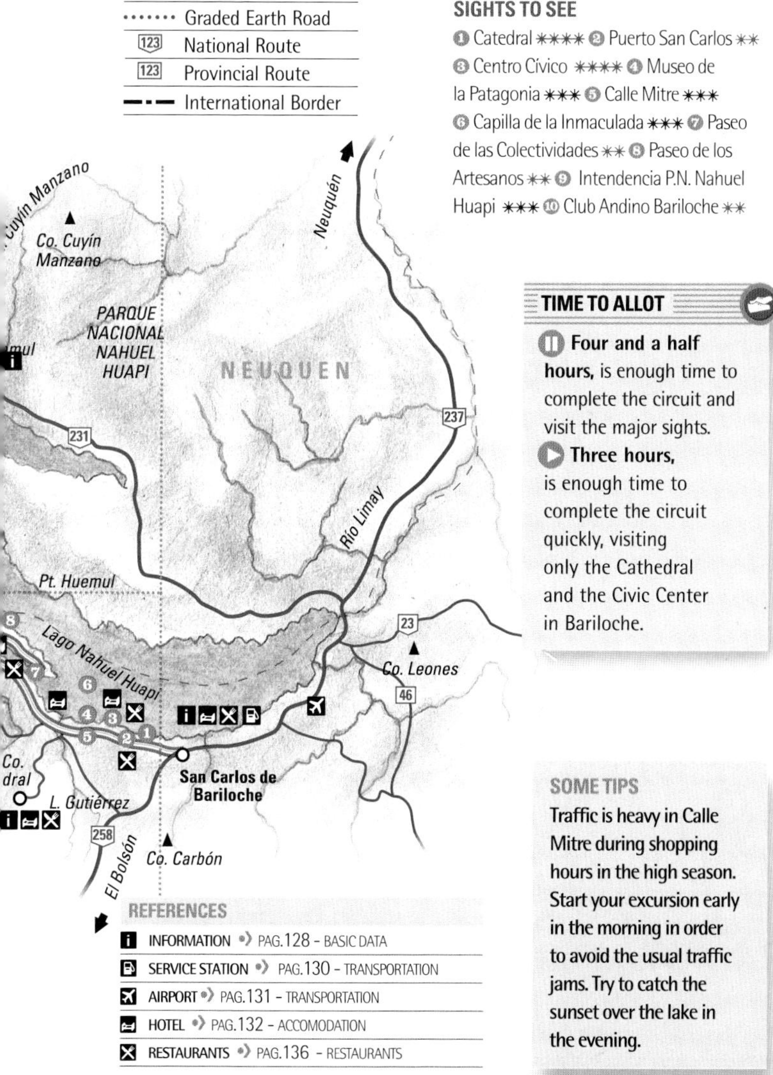

TIME TO ALLOT

Ⅱ **Four and a half hours,** is enough time to complete the circuit and visit the major sights.

▶ **Three hours,** is enough time to complete the circuit quickly, visiting only the Cathedral and the Civic Center in Bariloche.

SOME TIPS

Traffic is heavy in Calle Mitre during shopping hours in the high season. Start your excursion early in the morning in order to avoid the usual traffic jams. Try to catch the sunset over the lake in the evening.

REFERENCES

- INFORMATION ›› PAG.128 - BASIC DATA
- SERVICE STATION ›› PAG.130 - TRANSPORTATION
- AIRPORT ›› PAG.131 - TRANSPORTATION
- HOTEL ›› PAG.132 - ACCOMODATION
- RESTAURANTS ›› PAG.136 - RESTAURANTS

San Carlos de Bariloche

Located on the southern shores of Lake Nahuel Huapi, this town is the gateway to a beautiful region of lakes, rivers, snow-capped mountains and snowfields. Its importance as a tourist center grew gradually throughout the 20th century and, today it has become one of the areas with the most developed tourist infrastructure in Argentina.

❺ CALLE MITRE ✳✳✳

Principal shopping street, also admired for the harmonious style of its architecture.

THE ERRATIC ROCK

In front of the Cathedral there is a volcanic rock from the Quaternary period which was transported from the mountains to this site by a glacier.

❼ PASEO DE LAS COLECTIVIDADES ✳✳

PANOZZI
JURAMENTO
20 DE FEBRERO
MORALES
URQUIZA
O' CONNOR
QUAGLIA
PERITO MORENO
GENERAL VILLEGAS
BARTOLOME MITRE
AV. ELFLEIN

❿ CLUB ANDINO BARILOCHE ✳✳

Head offices of this traditional institution which pioneered mountain climbing in this city.

❻ CAPILLA DE LA INMACULADA ✳✳✳

A wooden chapel built in 1905.

❽ PASEO DE LOS ARTESANOS ✳✳

The area's principal crafts market is located in one of buildings on this avenue.

SIGHTS TO SEE

- CATEDRAL
- CENTRO CIVICO
- MUSEO DE LA PATAGONIA
- CALLE MITRE

FACTS

THE MYTH OF NAHUELITO
A legend tells of a prehistoric animal that lives in Lake Nahuel Huapi, similar to that of the Loch Ness Monster.

3 CENTRO CIVICO ✱✱✱✱
Traditional point of reference in Bariloche. he architecture of its stone buildings was inspired by the style of medieval constructions in the Alps.

4 MUSEO DE LA PATAGONIA ✱✱✱
Houses collections dealing with the nature and history of the Patagonian region.

2 PUERTO SAN CARLOS ✱✱
Point of departure for excursions on Lake Nahuel Huapi. Also includes a recreational area.

9 INTENDENCIA DEL PARQUE NACIONAL NAHUEL HUAPI ✱✱✱

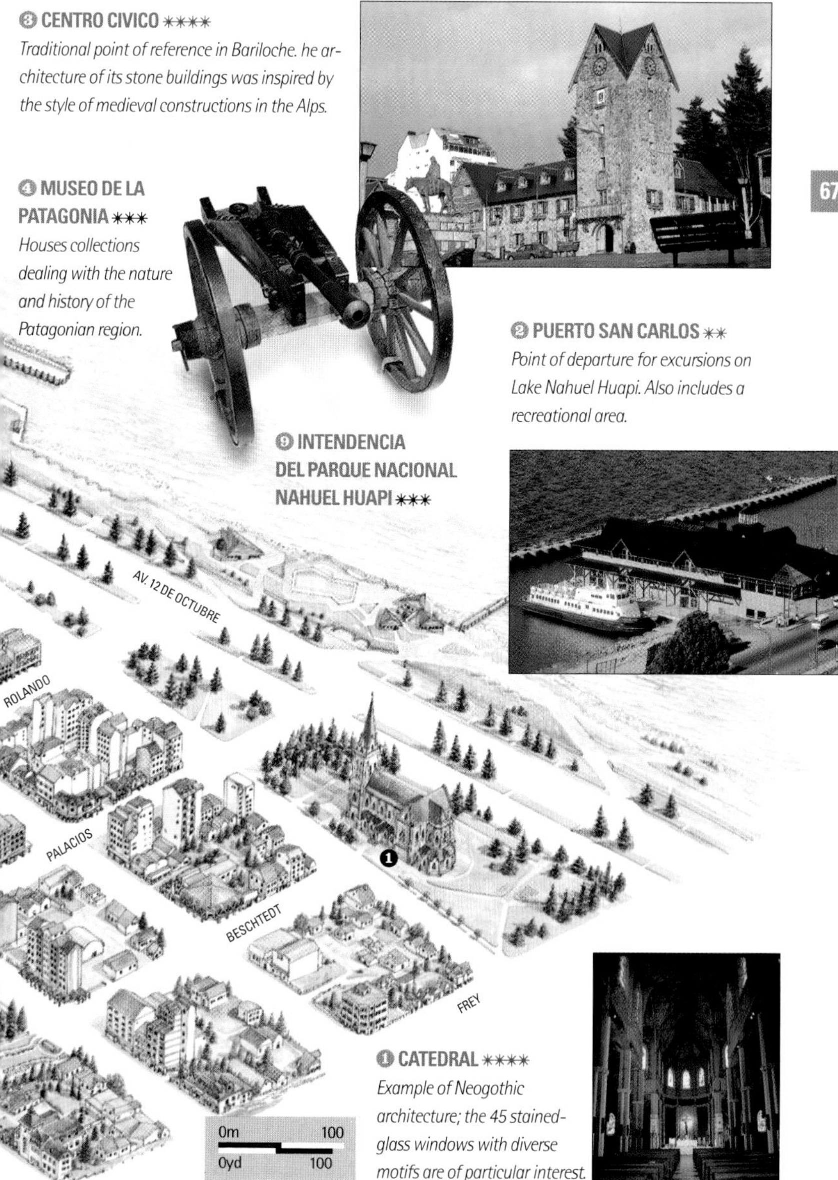

1 CATEDRAL ✱✱✱✱
Example of Neogothic architecture; the 45 stained-glass windows with diverse motifs are of particular interest.

This route starts on Avenida 12 de Octubre in Bariloche on the shores of the lake. The Cathedral can be see at the junction with Frey.

PRIMO CAPRARO

Capraro was one of the men behind Bariloche's building industry. He came to this region from Italy to prospect for gold, but when this project ended in failure he set up the basic workshop necessary for the construction of the first wooden houses in the town. He committed suicide in 1932.

CATEDRAL 1

Façade of the Cathedral in Bariloche.

Construction on the Neogothic Cathedral of Nuestra Señora de Nahuel Huapi was started in 1946 under the direction of the architect Alejandro Bustillo. The building is still unfinished, and to date only the central chapel has been completed. The interesting traditional stonework was carried out with stone from quarries near the city. The building has over 45 stained glass windows depicting religious themes and the history of Patagonia.

III 12 DE OCTUBRE AND PALACIOS.

▶ *On leaving the church take 12 de Octubre along the waterfront. Puerto San Carlos is about four blocks away after the parking lot.*

PUERTO SAN CARLOS 2

This is the embarkation point for boats offering excursions on Lake Nahuel Huapi. Here you can obtain information about excursions to Victoria Island and the myrtle woods of Puerto Quetrihué. This is also a stopping point for the modern catamarans that carry passengers to Huemul Island located just a few kilometers west of Bariloche. The port also boasts a cafeteria, an ice skating rink and a recreational area for children equipped with a hand ball court and ping-pong tables. In 1960 an earthquake whose epicenter was in the town of Valdivia (Chile) destroyed these facilities. They were rebuilt in 1989.

BONES AND INSECTS

The Paleontological Museum is located on Avenida Costanera y Sarmiento. The collection includes insects, frogs, snails, ferns, arachnids, and an enormous shark's jaw.

▶ *Cross 12 de Octubre. A small hill leads to the Plaza Expedicionarios del Desierto where the Civic Center is located.*

CENTRO CIVICO 3

Civic Center. This is the name given to a group of buildings constructed in the medieval style designed by the architect Ernesto Estrada in 1940. The complex is laid out around a small picturesque square ornamented with flowers and steps leading down to the water. In their materials and colors the buildings reflect the inspiration of the city of Berne, Switzerland. In the center of the

Boats offering excursions on Lake Nahuel Huapi leave from Puerto San Carlos.

The Centro Cívico in Bariloche is made up of important public buildings.

square is an equestrian statue of General Argentino Roca, one of the leaders of the Campaña del Desierto (Desert Campaign) famous for expelling the indigenous population from this area. The buildings that make up the Centro Cívico house local institutions such as City Hall, the Municipal Tourist Office, the Sarmiento Library, the Museo de la Patagonia, the police station, the Emilio Frey Exhibition Center, and a National Parks office. A clock tower on the City Hall displays symbolic images on the hour at 12.

MORE INFORMATION ON PAGES 70-71.

On the left with your back to the lake the Museo de la Patagonia is located in the building in the west wing of the square.

MUSEO DE LA PATAGONIA | 4

The Museo de la Patagonia.

The Patagonia Museum. This two-storey building houses a collection of dried flowers and fauna of the Patagonian region, archaeological pieces, native objects, military uniforms of the Campaña del Desierto, historical and iconographic documents, as well as old newspaper cuttings. The collection is divided into several sections dedicated to natural sciences, ethnography, pre-history, regional and local history.

MORE INFORMATION ON PAGES. 70-71.

On leaving the museum, the west side of Plaza Expedicionarios del Desierto is connected by arches with Calle Mitre.

CALLE MITRE | 5

Calle Mitre, a great shopping avenue.

This is the principal shopping street in the city. Here you will find most of the shops, shopping centers, cafes, chocolate shops , souvenir stands, regional products and restaurants. Many of its buildings have a similar architectural style, with wooden facades in the style of a mountain village, which are no higher than those of the Centro Cívico. This is due to an ordinance of the National Park that came into force in 1940.

TOURIST TRAIN

Since February 2001, Bariloche has had a steam train which travels from here to Perito Moreno, 30 kilometers away. This journey in a train pulled by an engine constructed in Scotland in 1912 is complemented by a lunch and a trek through the Patagonian steppes.

Centro Cívico of Bariloche

Civic Center. Built in 1940 and located in the heart of the city, this is the most important building in Bariloche, as it is home to the city's main government departments and offices. The buildings look a little like medieval Alpine constructions.

LAKE VIEW
Lake Nahuel Huapi is visible from several points in the Civic Center. The lake, which is right in front of the building, has a maximum depth of 218 m (715 ft).

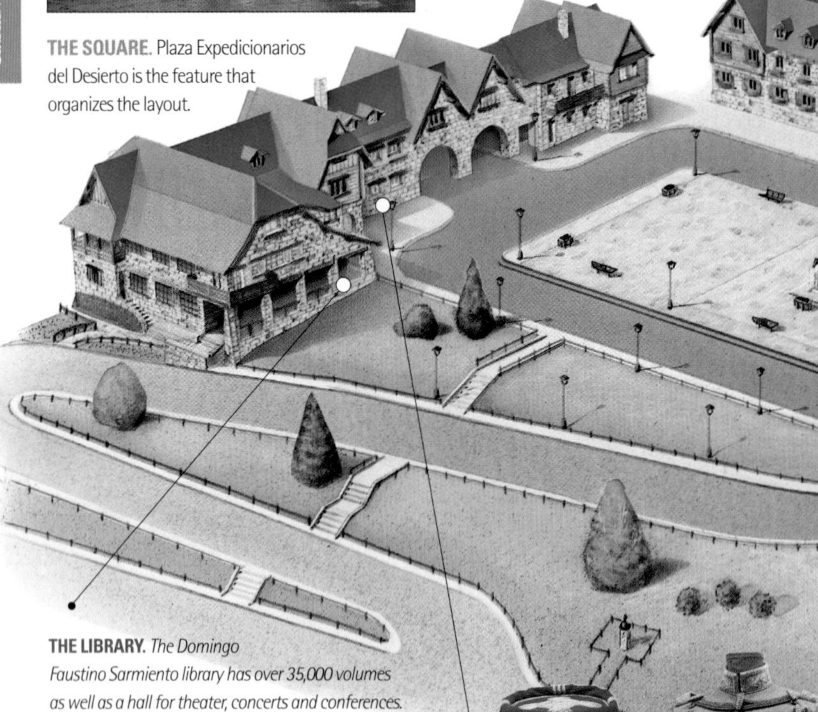

THE SQUARE. Plaza Expedicionarios del Desierto is the feature that organizes the layout.

THE LIBRARY. *The Domingo Faustino Sarmiento library has over 35,000 volumes as well as a hall for theater, concerts and conferences.*

THE UNIFORM worn by Colonel Lorenzo Vinter (commander of the Desert Expeditionary Force, 2nd Brigade) is on display in the Museum of Patagonia, along with preserved animals and historical, archeological and iconographic pieces.

USEFUL INFORMATION

ADDRESS: Avenida Mitre 305.

VISITS: The Museum of Patagonia is open Tuesday - Friday between 10 AM - 12:30 PM, and 2 PM - 7 PM. Saturdays: 10 AM -1 PM. The Secretaría Municipal de Turismo is open every day from 9 AM through 8 PM. The Domingo Faustino Sarmiento library is open Monday - Friday between 10 AM - 8 PM.

FACTS

SPECIAL STONE

The stone that was used to build the Centro Cívico was taken from a quarry near Cerro Carbón.

ERNESTO ESTRADA *was the architect who designed the Civic Center.*

SECRETARIA MUNICIPAL DE TURISMO at San Carlos de Bariloche is a harmonious combination of stone and slate, with wood sections such as the balustrade.

THE EMILIO FREYHALL, *next to the Police Station, is used for art and photography exhibitions.*

THE CLOCK TOWER above the City Hall contains figures of different famous local people who emerge when the clock strikes 12 noon.

THE STATUE *of General Julio A. Roca on horseback stands in the center of the square. He led the Desert Campaign.*

Five squares beyond the Civic Center, turn right off Mitre towards Beschtedt. The street gets steeper, and we climb up a flight of steps. The chapel is in the second square on the left..

CAPILLA DE LA INMACULADA | 6

The entrance of the Chapel of La Inmaculada.

Chapel. This is one of the oldest buildings in San Carlos de Bariloche. It was built on Calle Moreno by Primo Capraro, on commission from Father Zacarías Genghini. The original chapel, which had one single central nave, was completed on December 31st 1906. The lateral naves were added in 1951. In 1973, it was moved to its present location by sliding it up the side of the hill on rails. The exterior is surfaced with wooden slats, while wooden strips line the interior walls. A major renovation project was carried out on the building in 1981 – the interior flooring was removed and the slats on the façade and the altar were replaced. Next to the Chapel there is a marvelous lookout point with a view of the city center and the lovely cathedral of Nuestra Señora de Nahuel Huapi.

AV. EFLEIN ON THE CORNER WITH BECHSTEDT STREET.

Go back down Bechstedt, down the steps and turn left onto Moreno. Walk one block and you come to the Paseo de las Colectividades, a park.

THE FIRST SETTLER

Carlos Wiederhold is though to have been the first colonist to settle in Bariloche. He owned a large general store, around which he started building the first houses of Bariloche.

STUDENTS

Almost half the tourists that come to San Carlos de Bariloche every year are students. Since the 1970s, it has been a tradition for newly-graduated students to come here in April and November, to celebrate finishing their studies.

PASEO DE LAS COLECTIVIDADES | 7

This green space was designed as a tribute to all the countries from which the first city settlers came, and was made into a fully-equipped park in 1982. A bronze plaque to Perito Moreno was inaugurated in 1919, and there are a number of flagpoles flying the flags of all the different countries.

Continue in the same direction along Moreno. Three blocks further on, a wooden building on Villegas marks your arrival at the park Paseo de los Artesanos.

PASEO DE LOS ARTESANOS | 8

Building in Paseo de los Artesanos.

This park space includes a wooden building which houses the San Carlos de Bariloche Craft Market. Just like other such markets in the region, it sells souvenirs of the city, handcrafted items in wood, clothes, ceramics, postcards and all sorts of decorative items.

MORENO WITH VILLEGAS.

Carry on along Moreno two blocks in the same direction. After Morales, you'll see the Park Headquarters on the left.

A UNIQUE STYLE

Many buildings in San Carlos de Bariloche have a distinct architectural style, with large sloping roofs and lot of wood (Cypress and larch) used in the form of boards and slats. The "Bariloche style" came about through a local by-law passed several decades ago.

INTENDENCIA DEL P.N. NAHUEL HUAPI 9

Nahuel Huapi N.P Headquarters. Constructed in the 1940s, this stone and wood building is the headquarters of the biggest national park (710,000 hectares or 1,775 acres) in the whole Andean Patagonia lake corridor. Situated between Neuquén and Rio Negro provinces, the park stretches over a wide range of environments (high Andes, rain forest, transition vegetation and steppes). The park also has a number of archeological and historical sites and a large infrastructure. It has many large lakes (including Nahuel Huapi, Traful, Espejo, Gutiérrez and Mascardí), towns and cities (San Carlos de Bariloche, Villa La Angostura, Villa Traful and Villa Mascardí) and tourist centers. The park headquarters will give you all the information you need.

SAN MARTIN 24. TEL. (02944) 42-3111.

MORE ARCHITECTURE

Other buildings in Bariloche deserve a mention: the Capraro building (on Moreno with Urquiza), the Speranza house (on Moreno with Palacios) and the Oficina de Tierras y Colonias (on Elflein and Morales).

The headquarters of the Club Andino (Mountain sports club) is to the left of the park headquarters, one block along Morales and opposite the Law Courts.

The main façade of the Nahuel Huapi national park headquarters.

CLUB ANDINO BARILOCHE 10

The Club Andino Bariloche headquarters.

Bariloche Mountain Club. This was the first mountain sports institution created in the region. It was set up on August 13th 1931 by Emilio Frey, Juan Javier Neumeyer, Roberto Knapp and Otto Meiling. The building was designed by the architect Godofredo Haeker, who also built the adjoining house. Before construction, the small square on which the buisldinq stands was an artificial lake (a dam on the Molino River). There were a number of wooden access bridges and lush vegetation. The building was designed in the Alpine style, with small windows and a gently sloping roof. ■

20 DE FEBRERO AND MORALES.

Delicious Attractions

The local food products are just one more attraction of this region. Candies, liqueurs and smoked game and fish are the stars of the gastronomic show. The foods are all made using traditional recipes which were brought by the first settlers, and which have now become part of a prosperous industry.

▼ **EUROPEAN** women brought their recipes with them.

Sweet

▲ During the bitter winters, the Swiss colonists used to gather around the fireplace and enjoy jams and jellies made from wild fruits. Nowadays, these traditional methods of jam-making have become a successful industry.

▼ **PANCAKES.** Made with chocolate or local fruits such as strawberries, raspberries, morello cherries, redcurrants, blackberries and sweet brier.

Beer

▼ They have been making beer the traditional way in El Bolsón for the last 15 years, without using chemical products to replace the barley enzyme. The malt is boiled for six hours, after which it passes through different filtering and fermentation processes.

Smoked food

◄ In this region, a special method is used to cook trout, salmon, wild boar, deer and lamb. First they are cooked in salt, then they are hung at the top of a special cabinet, at the bottom of which there is a wood fire. The result is delicious.

FRUIT AND BERRIES IN EL BOLSÓN

The microclimate of the region on the 42nd parallel where El Bolsón is located is ideal for growing strawberries, raspberries, red currents, elderberries, sweet brier and other fruit. The land also produces tasty mushrooms that grow beneath pines and cypresses.

Curanto

Curanto is a peculiar way of cooking which involves burying the food together with hot stones in a hole dug in the ground.

▼**SHEEP'S CHEESE.** Ranches such as Belvedere, in El Bolsón make Peconino sheep's cheese. Also available marinated with herbs.

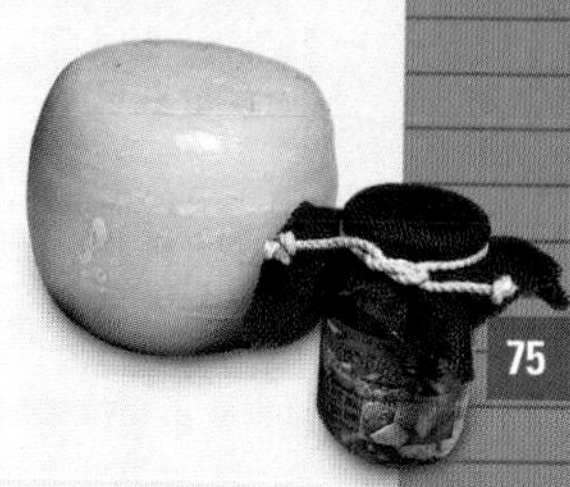

Chocolate

The world-famous Bariloche chocolate derives from recipes brought by Central European pioneers. It is refined in pans, melted to 36° C (96° F) and worked by hand into shapes such as tablets, individual chocolates and sticks, as well as marinated morello cherries dipped in chocolate and chocolate liqueurs.

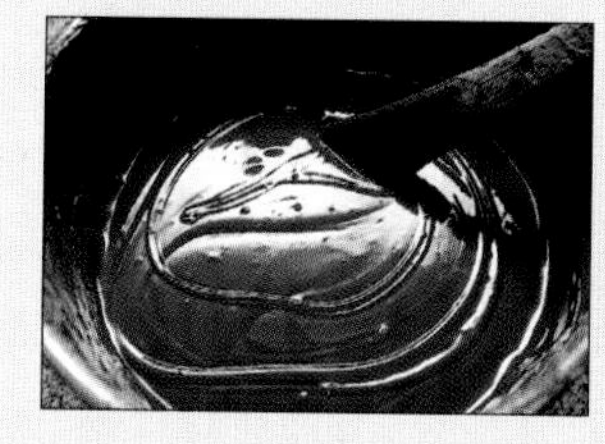

MULTI-FLAVOR. The chocolate makers use local fruit such as raspberries and redcurrants to give the chocolate different flavors.

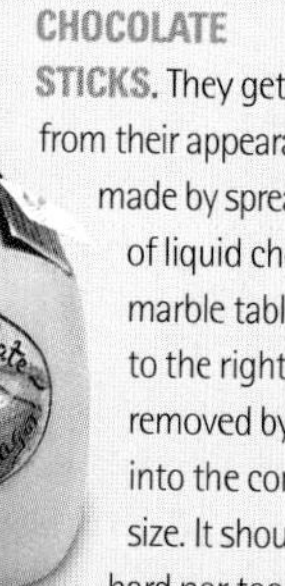

CHOCOLATE STICKS. They get their name from their appearance, and are made by spreading thin layers of liquid chocolate over a marble table. When it cools to the right temperature, it is removed by hand and worked into the correct shape and size. It should neither be too hard nor too full of bubbles.

Circuito Chico

The Short Circular Route. This 62-km-long circular route (with branch-offs) begins and ends in Bariloche. It runs along the shore of Nahuel Huapi and other lakes, past many excellent hotels, restaurants, lookout points, picnic areas, craft shops and green spaces. Visitors also have the option of taking boat trips or cable cars.

⑪ HOTEL LLAO LLAO ✱✱✱✱

This hotel, which stands in a beautiful setting, is one of the most prestigious in Argentina.

⑦ CERRO CAMPANARIO ✱✱✱

Has fantastic views of the landscape.

INSCRIPTIONS

- Asphalt Road
- Gravel Road
- Graded Earth Road
- 123 National Route
- 123 Provincial Route

⑨ CASA DE MUÑECAS ✱✱✱

This company produces beautiful handmade dolls and clocks.

⑧ CHOCOLATES FENOGLIO ✱✱

⑫ BAHIA LOPEZ ✱✱✱

Here you'll find rivers, woodland and one of the best lookout points on the route.

⑧ AHUMADERO FAMILIA WEISS ✱✱✱

Produces smoked salmon, venison and other delicacies.

⑬ COLONIA SUIZA ✱✱

Houses in the European style.

⑩ CAPILLA DE S. EDUARDO ✱✱✱

This wooden building looks down from a hilltop.

SIGHTS TO SEE

- THE CERRO OTTO CABLE CAR
- CERRO CAMPANARIO
- CAPILLA DE SAN EDUARDO
- HOTEL LLAO LLAO

FACTS

GREEN AREA

Llao Llao municipal park – on the peninsula of the same name – has paths, lookout points and campsites.

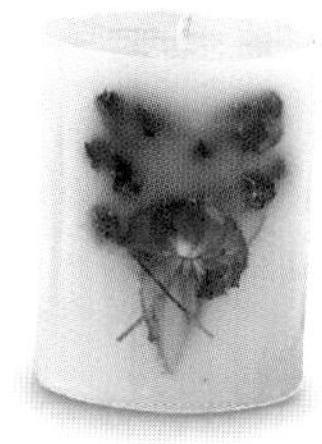

4 VELAS Y CERAMICAS BELEN **

One of several stores in the area where visitors can buy candles in all shapes and colors – like this one, which has a leaf cast inside it.

6 ISLA HUEMUL ***

Boat trips sail to this small island which, apart from its natural beauty, has an interesting history.

3 CLUB NAUTICO **

Regattas and races are organized here at different times through the year.

1 PARQUE CERRO VIEJO ***

Includes a number of eco-tourism routes, either on foot or by chair lift.

14 CERVECERIA BLEST **

Offers a wide range of beers and traditional German dishes.

5 CERRO OTTO CABLE CAR ***

Go and see the revolving café on the mountain top!

From the cathedral, take the street Juan Manuel de Rosas along the lakeside. After the Civic Center, the road joins Avenida Exequiel Bustillo. 1 km (0.6 miles) further on, you reach Cerro Viejo park, on your left.

PARQUE ECOTURISTICO CERRO VIEJO 1

Footpath in Cerro Viejo park.

Cerro Viejo Eco-Tourism. Opened in September 1998, this leisure park allows you to experience all the main features of natural beauty in the region without having to leave the old part of Bariloche city. The park stands at the foot of a mountain, and you can take a chair lift up to a peak 900 m high (2,952 ft.), where there is a café. There is also a botanic walk which includes examples of local flora such as Chile pines, coigues and other species. This path also has some carved wooden sculptures, a mountaineering museum in a cabin, a small myrtle forest and a 280 m (918 ft) slide.

III INFORMATION: TEL. (02944) 42-7644.

► *A little after the park – 1 km (a little over half mile) along Avenida Bustillo – there is a left turn to a chocolate factory.*

Patagonian fruit dipped in chocolate.

CHOCOLATES FENOGLIO 2

One of the best chocolate companies in Bariloche has its factory here, and you can take a guided tour to see all the processes of traditional chocolate-making. Fenoglio also has two retail outlets – on the streets Mitre and San Martín.

III AV. BUSTILLO KM 1,2.

► *Go along Avenida Bustillo. After 1 km (0.5 miles) there is a turnoff up to Cerro Otto. At the 3.6 km-point you will see the boats at the Yacht Club.*

LAKE VIEW

Go past the turnoff to the Fenoglio chocolate factory, and on the right you'll see the Nahuel Huapi lookout point, which has a lovely panoramic view of the lake and Huemul island.

CLUB NAUTICO 3

The Yacht Club. The club holds several regattas and competitions during the year, and also offers boat trips on the lake. The club has been here since 1976, as the original one – which had stood at Bariloche quay since 1947 – was destroyed by a violent earthquake in 1960.

III AV. BUSTILLO KM 3,6.

Boats moored at the Club Náutico.

► *Continue along Bustillo, and at the 4 km-point you reach the Belen candle and ceramics factory, one of several such companies in the area.*

VELAS Y CERAMICA BELEN 4

Candles and Ceramics. Here you can find traditional local handmade candles in different shapes, carved, perfumed or with leaves

Candles in different shapes and colors are produced all along the Circuito Chico.

Nahuel Huapi seen from the summit of Cerro Otto – and a paraglider in flight.

cast inside them. They can also be found at Velas Leo –a candle-making firm at the 15 km-point. Ceramics –in Central European styles– can also be found at Cerámicas Burton.

AV. BUSTILLO KM 4.

After Cerámicas Burton, a left turnoff at the 5 km takes you to the cable car up to Cerro Otto.

CERRO OTTO CABLE CAR 5

A cable railway goes from the foot of this mountain (named for the pioneer Otto Meiling) up to a revolving café 1,400 m high (4,593 ft). It has an excellent view. The whole circuit takes around 30 minutes.

AV. BUSTILLO KM 5.

Carry on along Av. Bustillo through a wood and on the right you pass a number of bungalows, hotels, houses and tea houses, such as the Hostería del Viejo Molino. At the 8 km-point there is a path off to Playa Bonita, right opposite Huemul island.

ISLA HUEMUL 6

Historical ruins on Huemul island.

Catamaran ferries sail from Puerto San Carlos to this island, where there are footpaths that take in features of natural and historical interest. Though it was declared a Historical, Ecological and Tourist park in 1994, the island had become famous in 1950 when the Austrian scientist Ronald Richter built a laboratory here to carry out research into controlled nuclear fission, a project promoted by President Peron.

Carry on past turnoffs to Cerro Catedral, the Chapel of San Ignacio, the Bariloche Atomic Center, Bahía Serena, the Jockey Club, and numerous stores and hotels. After Valle Escondido you reach the Cerro Campanario chair lift.

CERRO CAMPANARIO 7

The chair lift ground station has ample parking space. The chair lift will take you in a matter of minutes up to the top of the mountain, 1,050 m high (3,444 ft), where you can visit a famous café that has one of the best views of the serpentine Lake Nahuel Huapi, as well the Campanario channel and some other lakes.

AV. BUSTILLO KM 17,6.

TASTY DISHES

One of the many hotels in this section of the Circuito Chico, the exclusive hotel El Casco (at the 11.5 km-point-7 miles) is famed for its cuisine. The recipes of Ruth von Ellrichshausen – who co-founded the hotel in 1970 – have been published in several books.

20 km along Av. Bustillo (12.4 miles), a right turn leads to San Pedro peninsula. Take this road and after 1 km (0.6 miles) you reach the Ahumadero Familia Weiss.

AHUMADERO FAMILIA WEISS | 8

This firm produces traditional smoked venison, wild boar and trout, as well as the same foods in oil and brine. Smoked cheese is also available. The company belongs to the Weiss family, who have been manufacturing these products since 1983. The family also has a retail outlet in the center of Bariloche – "La Picada de la Familia Weiss" – where you can try their delicious products.

AV. BUSTILLO KM 20,3.

SAN PEDRO PENINSULA

At the 20 km-point there is a turnoff that takes you through dense forests; this area was discovered by the explorers Fonck and Hess, and surrounds the Campanario channel of Lake Nahuel Huapi.

Bustillo continues alongside the lake. Panoramic view at the 22.4 km-point. Right turnoff after 23.4 km leads to the Casa de Muñecas (Dolls' House).

CASA DE MUÑECAS | 9

Dolls' House. At La Casa de Muñecas y Relojes Del Monte they manufacture fine handmade china and wood pieces. They also sell handmade jointed dolls and clocks (with or without pendulum) made from larch wood, rauli and incense.

AV. BUSTILLO KM 23,4.

Beautiful collectors' doll.

1.5 km further (3 miles) on is a turnoff to the luxurious Hotel Tunquelén and a view of the mountains. The Chapel stands on a small hill at the 25 km-point.

CAPILLA DE SAN EDUARDO | 10

Chapel. This chapel was built in the 40's, funded by a donation from Juana G. de Devoto. It stands on a hill from where you have an excellent view of most of Villa Llao Llao. The chapel's restrained decor includes win-

The picturesque Chapel of San Eduardo.

dows decorated by the artist Marcos Jerman and a valuable painting by Raúl Soldi.

AV. BUSTILLO KM 25-POINT. MASS HELD SUNDAYS 11:30 AM JAN-FEB: MONDAY TO SUNDAY, 8 PM.

Go back onto Bustillo, which leads into the bay of Puerto Pañuelo; the left side is dominated by the shape of the Llao Llao.

HOTEL LLAO LLAO | 11

The sumptuous Hotel Llao Llao.

This hotel stands on a promontory between Lake Nahuel Huapi and Lake Moreno. It has a marvelous view of the epnoymous town that surrounds it and of the snowcapped Mt. Tronador, between the López and Capilla mountains. This hotel is the largest in San Carlos de Bariloche; it opened in 1938, and in 1993 was renovated and modernized, and now has 164 rooms

Smoked products from the Weiss family. Specialties are salmon, wild boar and cheese.

A LAKE JOURNEY TO CHILE

We recommend the lake boat trip from Puerto Pañuelo to Puerto Blest, at the western end of Nahuel Huapi. Here there are hotels, you can visit the Los Cántaros waterfall or take a trip out on Laguna Frías and onto the Pérez Rosales Pass in Chile.

and luxury suites, a tea room with a winter garden, a heated swimming pool and an 18-hole golf course. MORE INFORMATION ON PAGES 82 AND 134.

▶ *After entering Llao Llao municipal park, there are turnoffs to Villa Tacul and the Park Warden's post. View of Cerro Capilla at the 31 km-point; a little further on and you see the bay.*

BAHIA LOPEZ 12

The Alun Nehuen hotel is situated here, on Lake Nahuel Huapi. Bahía López has two excellent lookout points with views of the surrounding landscape, while the tiny Lago Escondido (Hidden lake) is just visible through the forest of coigues, radals, maitens, myrtles and culeas.

The views from the Bahía López lookout points are truly spectacular.

▶ *Cross the Angostura river. Lookout point at 35 km-point. After the López river, a right turnoff leads to Colonia Suiza.*

A sign in the Colonia Suiza area.

COLONIA SUIZA 13

The Swiss Colony. This is the area that was inhabited by the first Swiss settlers. They reached the region at the end of the 19th century, and raised cattle and grew barley and rye. The area has a great many picturesque wooden houses, as well as hotels and craft stores.

▶ *You can backtrack to get onto Bustillo (or go along the shore of Lake Moreno). When you get to the small lake El Trébol there is a turnoff to the brewery.*

CERVECERIA BLEST 14

Blest has excellent beers and food.

Traditional beer. This is where they brew most famous traditional beers in Argentina. In high season it's worth making a reservation before you go, as it is a very popular spot. They also serve delicious homemade pastries, pizza and traditional German specialties. ■

MORE INFORMATION ON PAGE 137.

▶ *After 2 km (1.2 miles), Bustillo rejoins the road at the turnoff point to Cerro Campanario (18 km) back to Bariloche.*

Hotel Llao Llao

This is the largest, most luxurious hotel in the area. Built by Alejandro Bustillo, it was opened in 1938 and completely renovated in 1993. It is built in a Canadian style with Norman tiles, cypress logs and exposed stonework, all of which blends with the surrounding natural landscape.

THE LOCATION was chosen by the architect Bustillo – up on a hill between Lakes Moreno and Nahuel Huapi, and with a wonderful view of the López, Capilla and Tronador mountains.

THE GOLF COURSE *with its 18 holes, was specially designed by Alberto Solar Dorrego.*

THE LOBBY is a cozy space which combines wood and stone, and features leather-upholstered chairs and elaborate chandeliers. Two enormous log fire-places take pride of place.

THE CUISINE *includes jams and pastries made using local fruit.*

USEFUL INFORMATION

ADDRESS: Av. Bustillo km 26.

VISITS: Non guests can take a 20-minute guided tour of the building and the facilities. Please phone beforehand: (02944) 44-8530.

GUIDED TOURS: Mondays, Thursdays and Sundays (though tours may not take place on certain days).

FACTS

PRESIDENTIAL VISIT

When Dwight Eisenhower, President of the United States visited Argentina in 1961, he stayed at the Hotel Llao Llao.

THE CONFERENCE ROOM *is equipped with all the latest technology for meetings, cultural activities, courses and conferences.*

THE HEATED POOL *is part of the hot springs installation. Everything you need to relax.*

THE ORIGINAL MENU *from the inauguration (1938) is in the Museum of Patagonia.*

THE PRESIDENTIAL SUITE has a living room, a dining room with a wood fire, a bathroom with a Jacuzzi, and a kitchen, as well as an enormous balcony with a panoramic view.

THE WINTER GARDEN is a place for eating, drinking tea or simply for relaxing in comfortable wicker chairs on thick carpets, while enjoying the view of Lake Nahuel Huapi.

Bosque de Arrayanes and Isla Victoria

This boat trip stops off at two of the main attractions at Lake Nahuel Huapi – a walk through the magical Bosque de Arrayanes (Myrtle forest) and a visit to Victoria island, which is rich in history and natural beauty.

❸ ISLA VICTORIA ★★★★

Places of interest:

- Sendero Playa del Toro
- Sendero Cerro Bella Vista
- Sendero de las Sequoias

INSCRIPTIONS

▬▬	Asphalt Road
═══	Gravel Road
•••••••	Graded Earth Road
123	National Route
123	Provincial Route

Peninsula Quetrihue

BOSQUE DE ARRAYANES ❷

Puerto Quetrihue

ISLA VICTORIA

Peninsula Llao Llao

❷ BOSQUE DE ARRAYANES ★★★★

Take a walk (approx. 1 hour) along a path through a forest which is absolutely unlike any other – the height, color and unusual shapes of the myrtle trees make it a spectacular experience.

BIGGEST ISLAND

With a surface area of 3,700 hectares (20 km long and 4 km across at its widest point - 12.4 x 2.4 miles), Victoria Island is the largest island in Lake Nahuel Huapi.

SIGHTS TO SEE

- PUERTO PAÑUELO
- BOSQUE DE ARRAYANES
- CERRO BELLA VISTA FOOTPATH
- SENDERO PLAYA DEL TORO

FACTS

MIXED WOODLAND

Sequoias, firs, eucalyptus, ash trees, birch and other species have been introduced onto Victoria island as part of a reforestation plan.

The Sequoia path takes you past tall, majestic trees. *(Isla Victoria).*

Playa Nevada and restaurant in the back-ground, on the Playa del Toro path.*(Isla Victoria).*

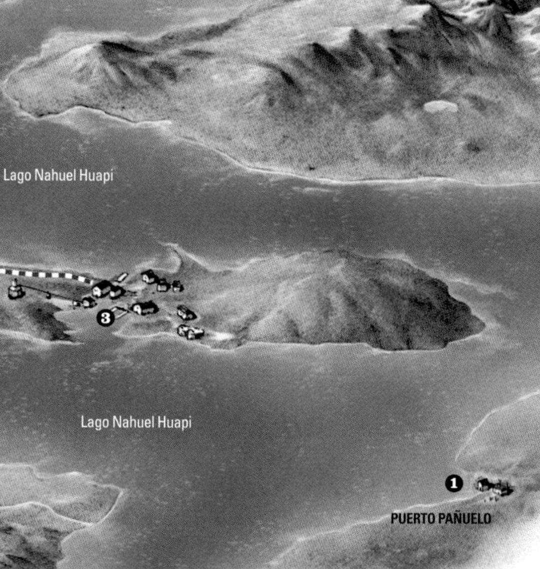

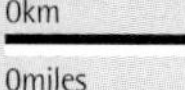

LOST A LETTER

The name originally given to the island in 1884 was Isla Victorica. A transcription error gave the island its present name of Victoria.

1 PUERTO PAÑUELO ★★

This is the starting point for the boat trip around Nahuel Huapi, the largest lake in the region, to visit the Myrtle forest and Victoria island.

This sector begins 26 km west (16 miles) from Bariloche, at Puerto Pañuelo, the most important harbor for lake trips.

PUERTO PAÑUELO 1

The boat trip from Puerto Pañuelo to Puerto Quetrihue (on the peninsula of the same name) takes approximately one hour, with magnificent views of the surrounding landscape followed by a walk through the Myrtle forest. Boats also leave from Puerto Pañuelo for Puerto Anchorena, on Victoria island.

INFORMATION: TEL. (02944) 42-6109.

View of Puerto Pañuelo bay.

The catamaran to Puerto Quetrihue takes around an hour. From there you can get to Bosque de Arrayanes (the Myrtle forest).

Traditional farmhouse in the Myrtle forest, near Puerto Quetrihue.

BOSQUE DE ARRAYANES 2

The Myrtle Forest. The footpath through the Myrtle forest is 600 m (1,968 ft) of wooden walkway and steps. Myrtles are generally a solitary bush-like species that grows to a height of 5m elsewhere in South America, and it is only here that they grow as trees, reaching heights of 18 m (59 ft) – and with some 25 m (82 ft) in height. The trees in this forest are up to 300 years old, and grow alongside other species such as the coigue and the cypress.

MORE INFORMATION ON PAGE 88-89

After the 45-minute walk, we board the boat one again and sail to Puerto Anchorena (approx. 30 mins.), also on Victoria island. Several footpaths start from this harbor.

OLD SCHOOL

The old southern Park Warden's School is situated in the Puerto Gross area. The school moved location years ago, and the building is not currently in use.

CAVE PAINTINGS

Leave Puerto Anchorena on the Playa del Toro path and after 500 m you come to a series of red and black cave paintings. Research shows that they were made by the Tehuelche people some 500 years ago.

ISLA VICTORIA 3

This is the largest island on the lake (3,710 hectares / 9,275 acres), and it is divided into three sectors: north, south and central. The latter sector is the only one with a tourist infrastructure, as building is prohibited on the others. The island contains many different newly-introduced tree species, such as tujas, birch, ash, eucalyptus and pines. The indigenous fauna includes the Bandurria ibis, the woodpecker and the pygmy owl.

SENDERO PLAYA DEL TORO ①

Footpath. This path takes approximately 45 minutes. Leave Puerto Anchorena to the right, stop to take a look at the cave paintings, followed by the look-out point with a view across the bay. Presently you reach Playa del Toro, where there is a café serving meals.

AARON DE ANCHORENA'S HOUSE

A path leads off left from Puerto Anchorena through a pine wood. After a few minutes you reach Puerto Grosso, where an old wooden house stands; this used to belong to Aarón de Anchorena, the first white man to settle on Victoria island, at the start of the 20th century. Anchorena built a number of houses, a sawmill, storehouses and corrals. He also introduced different species such as wild boar, deer and pheasants, and exchanged goods with the local tribes.

Café at Playa del Toro.

SENDERO CERRO BELLA VISTA ②

Footpath. The Cerro Bella Vista path goes up a fairly sharp gradient, and takes about an hour, going up through coigue and cypress woodland as far as the peak of Cerro Bella Vista, which offers a beautiful view of the island and Lake Nahuel Huapi.

Another way of seeing the island from on high is by taking the chair lift. At the lower chair lift station you can choose from a wide variety of food and handicrafts, or go visit one of the regular exhibitions of photography that are put on here.

There are some beautiful views from the peaks of Victoria island.

SENDERO DE LAS SEQUOIAS

The path runs through lofty woodland.

Footpath. This footpath, which also starts at Puerto Anchorena, takes around 30 minutes, and includes a few gentle gradients. It runs through a tall forest that includes such exotic species as pines, sequoias, firs, cedars, oaks and birch trees. Nearby stands the old National Nurseries, which opened in 1925 but has now closed down. ■

Bosque de Arrayanes

The Myrtle Forest. This unique forest stands on the Quetrihue peninsula, on land that used to belong to Antonio M. Lynch. It is now a National Monument, and a permanently protected area. There are few other places in the world where you can see these lovely trees with their attractive cinnamon-colored bark.

UNIQUE is the only word to describe these myrtles. Elsewhere they exist in the form of solitary shrubs, but here they have grown into trees.

STRANGE SHAPES *caught in the sunlight filtered through the branches.*

ACCESS to the forest: either take the catamarans that sail from Puerto Pañuelo or take the track from Villa La Angostura which crosses the Quetrihue peninsula.

THE UNDERGROWTH *is protected to encourage tree growth.*

ANCIENT TREES

The average age of these myrtles is thought to be between 150 and 250 years old, though some have reached 600 years.

USEFUL INFORMATION

VISITS: Boats to the forest leave from Puerto Pañuelo (26 km along Av Bustillo – 16 miles) – or take the 12-km (7.4-mile) track from Villa La Angostura harbor.

GUIDED TOURS: The whole-day trip to Victoria Island and the Myrtle forest leaves Puerto Pañuelo at 10 A.M. and returns at 5 P.M.

FACTS

REPRODUCTION

Myrtles reproduce from their flowers, as well as from the shoots that grow out of their roots and the branches that fall to the ground.

THE HEIGHT *of the trees on the Quetrihue peninsula is around 18 m (59 ft), though some reach 25 m (82 ft) – this occurs nowhere else in the world.*

A FOOTPATH on a 600 m circular route (660 yards), with wooden walkway and steps, takes visitors through the Myrtle forest. Straying off the path is strictly prohibited.

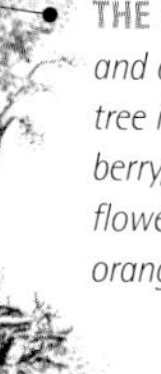

THE LEAVES *are small, perennial and aromatic. The fruit of the tree is a tiny violet berry, and its flowers resemble orange blossom.*

THE BARK is cinnamon-colored due to its tannin content. It comes off in strips, leaving white marks on the trunk.

THE FOREST CABIN *is a log house that stands amidst the trees – a welcome break in the walk, where you can have refreshments and browse through souvenirs and handcrafted items.*

The Lord of the Parks

The conservation of natural spaces in Argentina all started in Andean Patagonia. After experiencing the beauty of the southern lakes and mountains, Perito Francisco Moreno began to promote the conservation of the area in the early 20th century. Soon others joined in the work of protecting the land.

Nahuel Huapi

◄ On November 6th 1903, Perito Moreno donated 3 leagues (225 square km - 139 square miles) out of the 25 that the government granted him near Nahuel Huapi in order to create a national park.

► **ALTIMETER** from the 19th century which belonged to the politician Adolfo Alsina.

The First Scientists

▼ During the 1879 Desert Campaign, engineers and topographers traveled with the troops to chart the Patagonian terrain. It was they who made the first scientific studies of the area.

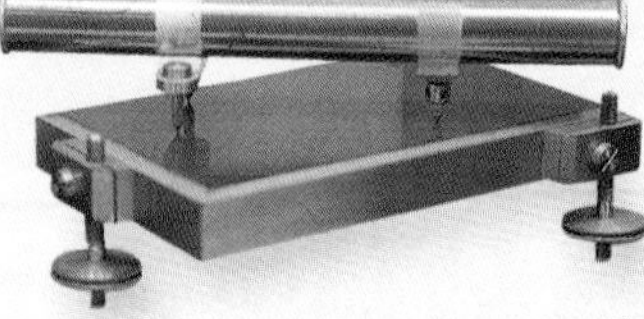

▲ **INSTRUMENTS** used by the pioneers exploring the area – such as this level and these binoculars – are now in the Museum of Patagonia.

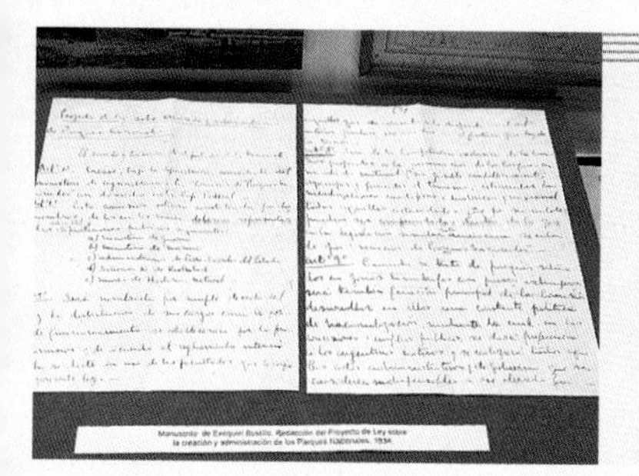

BUSTILLO'S MANUSCRIPT
The National Parks Law was passed in 1934. The architect Exequiel Bustillo, the first president of this organization, drafted the manuscript of the regulations. He held the post for ten years.

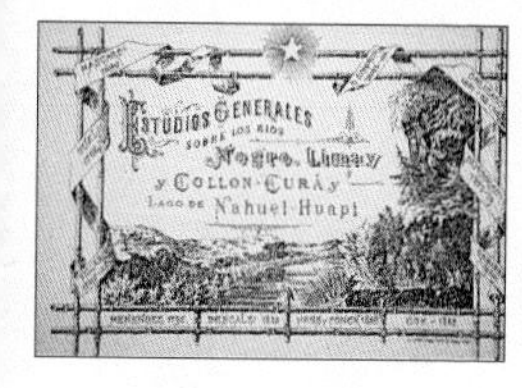

◀ **STUDIES** on the Negro, Lima and Collón Cura rivers preceded the creation of the national parks.

▶ **DOCUMENTS.** Right: a telegram sent by Perito Moreno and a letter asking the Mendoza and San Luís governments for support.

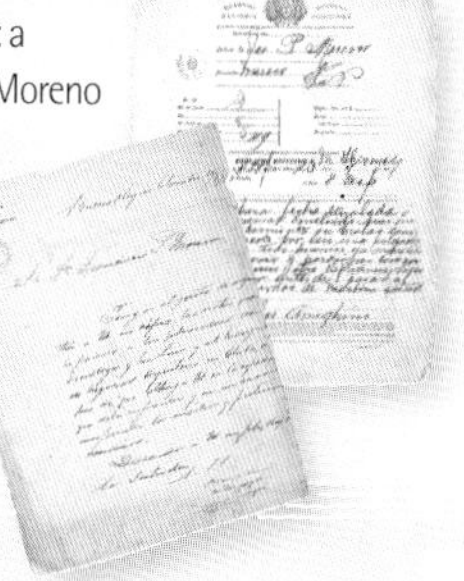

▲ **THE AIM FOR THE PARKS.** The initial aim of the National Park Administration (above, 1937 poster for Nahuel Huapi national park), apart from promoting high-class tourism, was to consolidate and encourage land colonization.

Perito Moreno

▶ Perito Francisco Moreno went south for the first time in 1873. He made several explorations of northern and southern Patagonia, when the area was still dominated by the Indians. A great traveler, he was an arbitrator in border conflicts, he set up scientific commissions, founded the La Plata Museum of natural science and initiated the creation of Nahuel Huapi park.

THE THEODOLITE was an important instrument for scientists, who used it to calculate the topography.

THE REMAINS of Perito Moreno are buried on Centinela Island, in Lake Nahuel Huapi.

Adventures in the Snow

The highlights of this itinerary – which runs through thick woodland, rivers with rapids, glaciers and beautiful lakes – are two high mountains: Cerro Catedral, a leading national ski center, and Cerro Tronador, very popular with climbers.

MONTE TRONADOR

VENTISQUERO NEGRO

ROCA LAKE

CATEDRAL SKI CENTER

CAÑA COLIHUE

LOS ALERCES WATERFALL

ITINERARY 4

LOOKOUT POINT OVER LAGO MASCARDI
VILLA CERRO CATEDRAL
MANSO RIVER
CHAPEL OF VIRGEN DE LAS NIEVES
VENTISQUERO NEGRO GLACIER
MASCARDI LAKE

Cerro Catedral to Monte Tronador

This itinerary includes two of the largest mountains in the area. The first part of the route leaves from Bariloche and goes up to the Catedral ski center, one of the largest on the continent. The route then descends to Gutiérrez, the first of the two big lakes. It continues through woodland and leisure are as as far as the v-shaped Lake Mascardi, before rising again to an icefield and the massive Monte Tronador.

Sector 1
CERRO CATEDRAL AND LAKE GUTIERREZ

SIGHTS TO SEE

❶ Capilla de la Virgen de las Nieves ✱✱ ❷ Centro de Salmonicultura Bariloche ✱✱ ❸ Villa Cerro Catedral ✱✱✱✱ ❹ Catedral Ski Center ✱✱✱✱ ❺ Lake Gutiérrez ✱✱✱

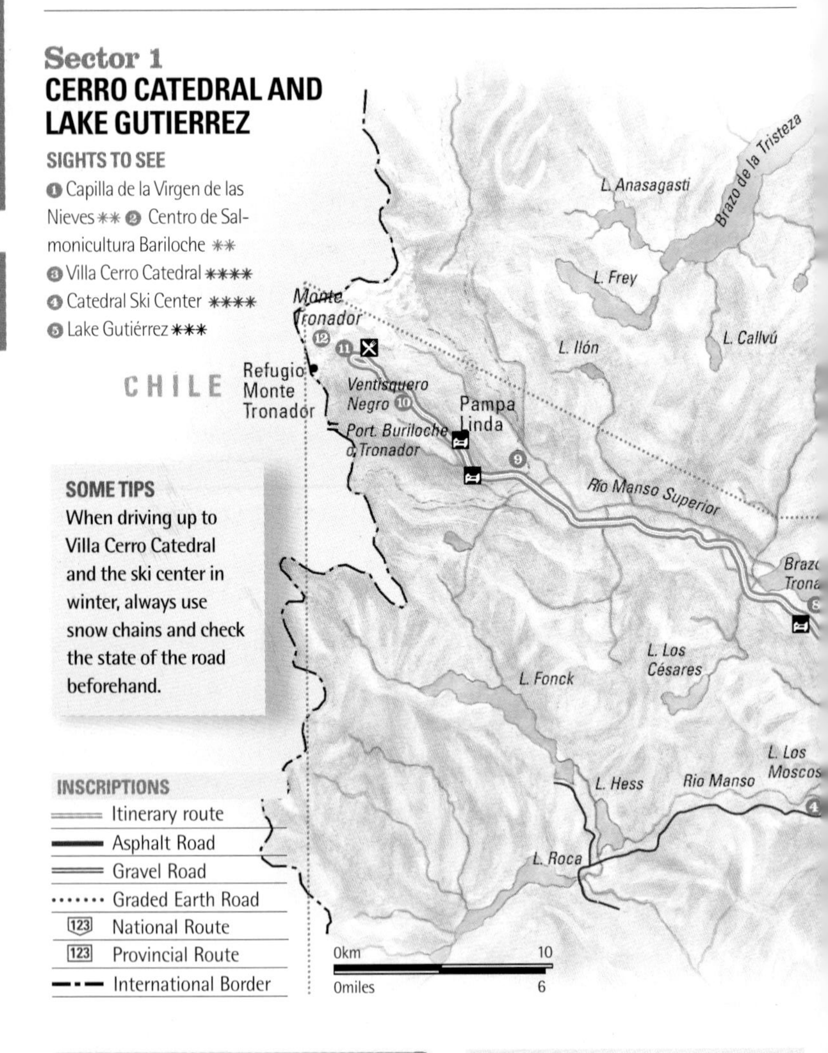

SOME TIPS

When driving up to Villa Cerro Catedral and the ski center in winter, always use snow chains and check the state of the road beforehand.

INSCRIPTIONS

- Itinerary route
- Asphalt Road
- Gravel Road
- Graded Earth Road
- 123 National Route
- 123 Provincial Route
- International Border

TIME TO ALLOT

Two days, enough to spend one at the ski center and another on Lake Gutiérrez.

Five hours, is enough to see Villa Cerro Catedral and go to Gutiérrez.

REFERENCES

INFORMATION » PAGE 128 - BASIC DATA
SERVICE STATION » PAGE 130 - TRANSPORTATION
AIRPORT » PAGE 131 - TRANSPORTATION
HOTEL » PAGE 132 - ACCOMMODATION
RESTAURANTS » PAGE 136 - RESTAURANTS

TIME TO ALLOT	Detailed visit: three days. Rapid visit: two days.
DISTANCE	130 km approx. (80 miles)
MEANS	By car and on foot.

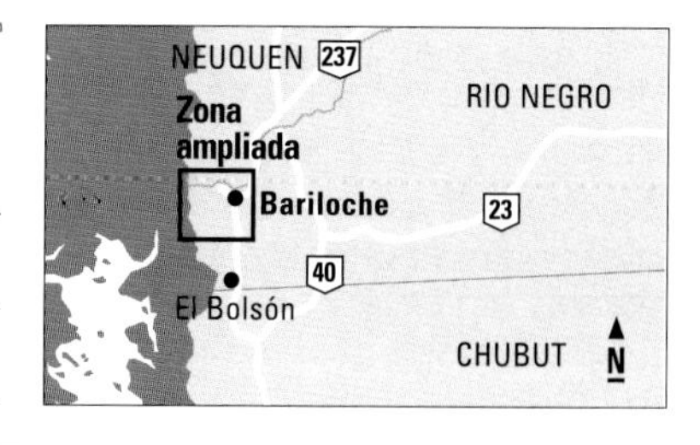

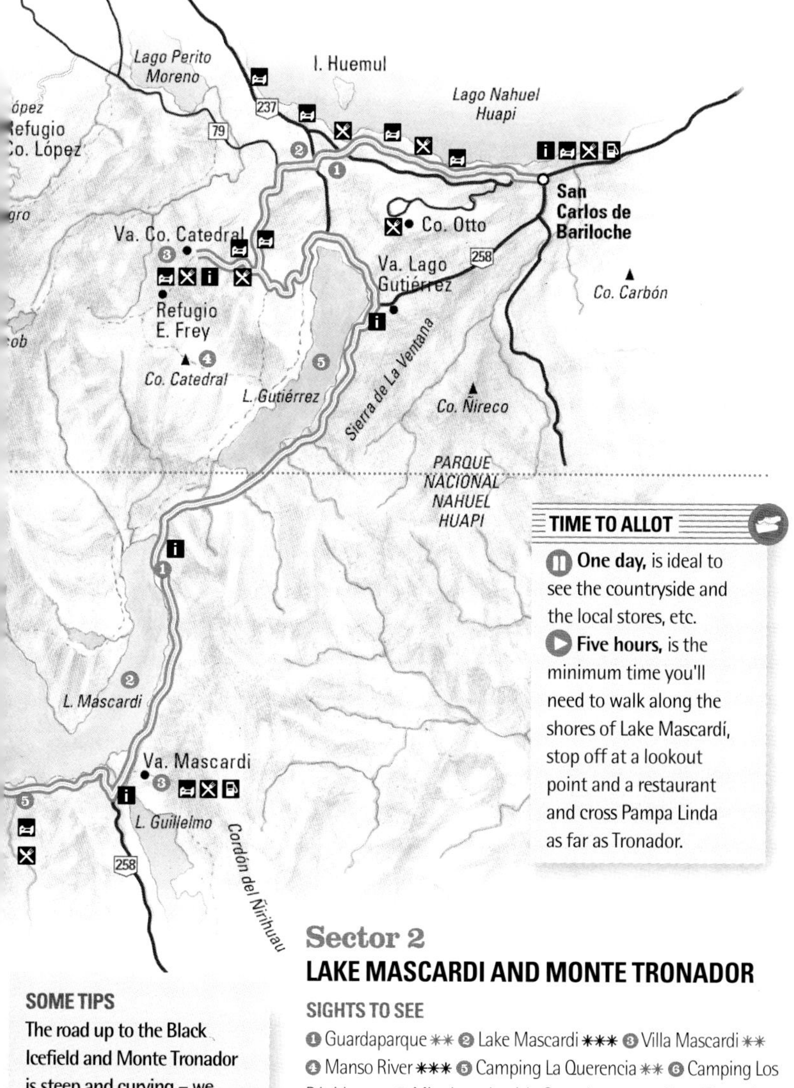

TIME TO ALLOT

One day, is ideal to see the countryside and the local stores, etc.

Five hours, is the minimum time you'll need to walk along the shores of Lake Mascardí, stop off at a lookout point and a restaurant and cross Pampa Linda as far as Tronador.

SOME TIPS

The road up to the Black Icefield and Monte Tronador is steep and curving – we recommend using an off-road vehicle in winter.

Sector 2
LAKE MASCARDI AND MONTE TRONADOR

SIGHTS TO SEE

❶ Guardaparque ✱✱ ❷ Lake Mascardi ✱✱✱ ❸ Villa Mascardi ✱✱ ❹ Manso River ✱✱✱ ❺ Camping La Querencia ✱✱ ❻ Camping Los Rápidos ✱✱ ❼ Mirador sobre isla Corazón ✱✱✱ ❽ Hotel Tronador ✱✱✱ ❾ Pampa Linda ✱✱✱ ❿ Ventisquero Negro ✱✱✱ ⓫ Hostería Los Ventisqueros ✱✱ ⓬ Monte Tronador ✱✱✱.

Cerro Catedral and Lake Gutiérrez

The route goes from Bariloche along the Circuito Chico as far as a turnoff leading to a chapel and a salmon farm. It then curves upwards to the unmissable Catedral ski center, before descending to the beautiful Lake Gutiérrez.

❹ CATEDRAL SKI CENTER ✱✱✱✱

The best of its kind in South America in terms of size and services.

Cerro Catedral

❹

Cerro Catedral Sur

258

Okm 2
Omiles 1

INSCRIPTIONS

——	Asphalt Road
══	Gravel Road
·······	Graded Earth Road
123	National Route
123	Provincial Route

❸ VILLA CERRO CATEDRAL ✱✱✱✱

This tourist resort lies at the foot of Catedral ski center, and includes a wide range of hotels and leisure activities.

SIGHTS TO SEE

- CAPILLA DE LA VIRGEN DE LAS NIEVES
- CENTRO DE SALMONICULTURA
- CATEDRAL SKI CENTER
- LAKE GUTIERREZ

FACTS

SKIING HISTORY

The first Argentina Ski Championships were held on Cerro Catedral in 1941.

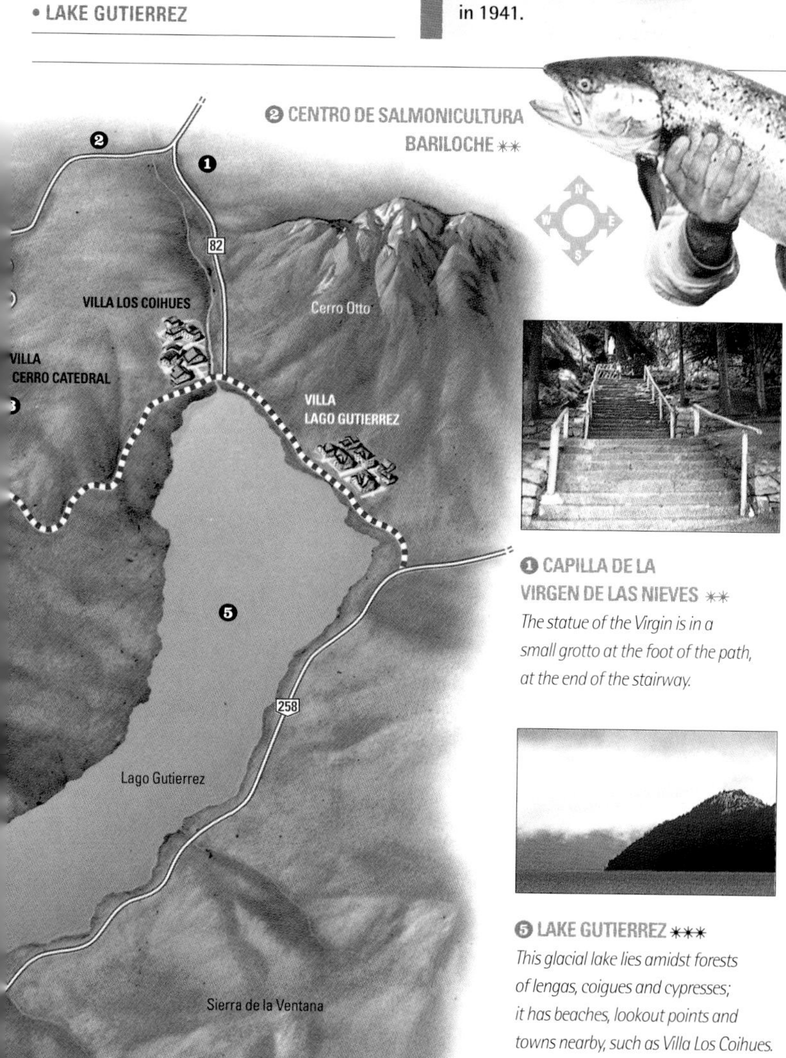

❷ CENTRO DE SALMONICULTURA BARILOCHE ✳✳

❶ CAPILLA DE LA VIRGEN DE LAS NIEVES ✳✳

The statue of the Virgin is in a small grotto at the foot of the path, at the end of the stairway.

❺ LAKE GUTIERREZ ✳✳✳

This glacial lake lies amidst forests of lengas, coigues and cypresses; it has beaches, lookout points and towns nearby, such as Villa Los Coihues.

CABLE CAR UP THE MOUNTAIN

The cable car, which was installed in 1950, is the oldest method of getting up to Catedral ski center.

Take Av. Bustillo out of Bariloche, and at the 8.5 km-point take a left turn around the barracks. View of Cerro Catedral. At the 11 km there is another left turn in front of a dam. On the other side of the road stands the Chapel of the Virgin.

This wooden building is the Villa Cerro Catedral ski school.

CAPILLA DE LA VIRGEN DE LAS NIEVES 1

Chapel. The sacred statue of the "Virgin of the Snows" is located in a small stone cave, at the end of a sign-posted stone stairway. Offerings, candles and engraved plaques in honor of the virgin are displayed along the stairway.

► *If you did not take the previous turn opposite the dam, carry on over a bridge across the Gutiérrez river. Soon you see a turn on the right to the Centro de Salmonicultura de Bariloche.*

CENTRO DE SALMONICULTURA DE BARILOCHE 2

Bariloche Salmon Farm. The Centro de Salmonicultura de Bariloche was opened in 1904. The salmon farm was originally located on a small river east of San Carlos De Bariloche, but in 1933 the farm moved to the point where the rivers La Cascada and Gutiérrez converge. At the farm they specialize in salmon dispersion and acclimatization, and the production of trout roe and fry.

III ROAD TO CERRO CATEDRAL KM 11. VISISTS: MONDAY THROUGH FRIDAY, FROM 9 AM TO 6 PM.

► *An asphalt road curves upwards past some beautiful views, and in 20 minutes you arrive at Villa Cerro Catedral.*

GOTHIC CATHEDRAL

The mountain was given the name "Catedral" because of the curious shape of its peaks, which resemble a gothic-style cathedral.

VILLA CERRO CATEDRAL 3

This tourist resort – just like Villa Llao Llao and Villa La Angostura – was built in a national park to attract tourism to the Andean mountain chain. The rising popularity of skiing led to the creation of the Club Andino de Bariloche in 1931, as well as several ski clubs. Catedral chapel, which is made out of stone and contains a bronze figure of the Madonna by Dolomitti, is particularly worth visiting.

► *The Villa Cerro Catedral complex, with its hotels, clubs and shopping centers, stands at the foot of the ski slopes.*

OVER 2,000 SETS OF SKIS

Los Troncos, El Establo and Las Terrazas are the three stores where you can hire equipment for up to 2,000 skiers – all types of skis and a total of 200 snowboards.

CATEDRAL SKI CENTER 4

The ski center, which stands on the west side of Cerro Catedral, is the biggest in South America. It was built during the 1960s, after skiing had become popular following the championships that were held there. The 200-hectare area of skiable mountainside includes 67 km (41.6 miles) of slopes and lifts, including the Robles and Ladobueno chair lifts, 17 ski lifts, 2 babylifts, 1 cable car, 2 carrousels and 1 drag lift. There are a number of bars, restaurants, shelters, cafes and kiosks where you can take a break on your way down.

•› MORE INFORMATION ON PP. 100 - 101.

▸ *You can either go down a gravel road, or go back to the turnoff by the Chapel and follow the asphalt road. Both routes lead to Lake Gutiérrez.*

A view of Villa Cerro Catedral, at the foot of the Catedral ski center slopes.

LAKE GUTIERREZ 5

This glacial lake lies 12 km (7.4 miles) from San Carlos de Bariloche, between the Ventana mountain range and Cerro Catedral. The river Gutiérrez connects it to Lake Nahuel Huapi, and the lake is surrounded by thick woodland (mostly coihue, lenga and cypress trees). The waters contain fish such as brook trout, rainbow trout and brown trout. ■

Quay on Lake Gutiérrez.

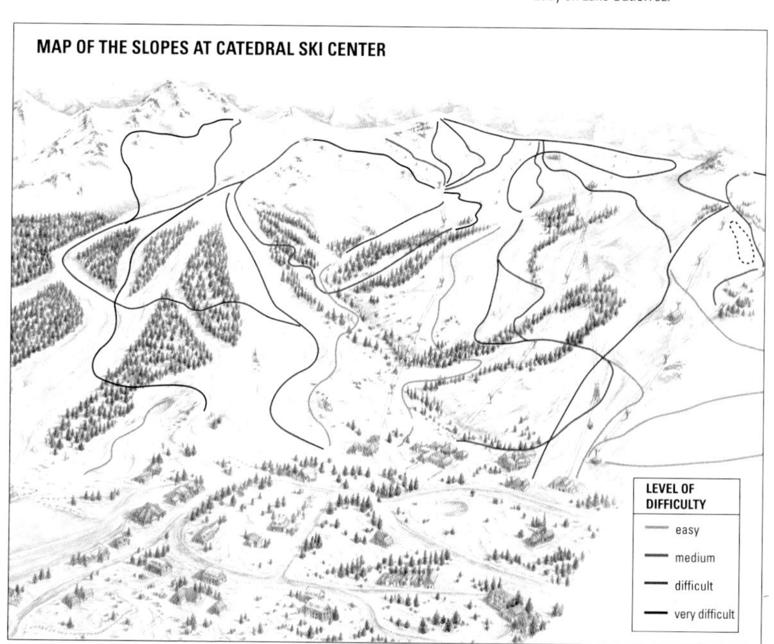

Cerro Catedral

Catedral Alta Patagonia, only a few kilometers away from San Carlos de Bariloche, is one of the largest ski centers in South America, and together with Villa Cerro Catedral (at the foot of the slopes) represents a leisure and service infrastructure which can deal with thousands of winter sports enthusiasts.

HOTEL & CATERING. Cerro Catedral has excellent apartments and superb restaurants.

MOUNTAINS. *Negro, Punto Nevada and other peaks surround the center.*

DIFFERENT SLOPES *for different levels of ability. International competitions have also been held here.*

LAS TERRAZAS SHOPPING CENTER, 25,590 sq. feet in size, with three stories of shops, terrace areas, an auditorium, a kindergarten and 4,000 decorative plants.

ALL YEAR *visitors can go walking, horse-riding, cycling, off-road driving and climbing.*

USEFUL INFORMATION

ADDRESS: Villa Cerro Catedral, s/n.
Information: tel. (02944) 46-0125.

HOURS: the ski lift runs all year from 8:30 a.m. in winter (earlier during the summer), to 5 p.m hours.

VISITS: the ski center is open all year for one-day trips or longer stays.

FACTS

GOING FLAT-OUT
Special machines compact the snow on the slope, working at up to 45 hectares per hour.

CONSTRUCTION of the ski center began in 1938. The first hotel opened in 1944 and the cable car was added in 1950.

SKI LIFTS *carry a maximum of six persons at a time, traveling the whole slope circuit in under 10 minutes.*

SURFING. *The first snowboard park in South America was opened at Cerro Catedral in 1997.*

AT THE FOOT OF THE SLOPES, *there is a large square with hotels, cafes, teahouses and restaurants.*

SKIS *can be repaired, hired or bought at El Establo, Los Troncos or Las Terrazas.*

Lake Mascardi and Monte Tronador

The huge V-shaped Lake Mascardí, with its crystal-clear water, can be seen from most points in this sector. It has campsites, beaches and lookout points, plus a lovely walk through forests and flatland to a glacier and to the foot of Monte Tronador.

8 HOTEL TRONADOR ✱✱✱
Founded in 1929 by the Belgian family Vereertbrugghen, this wooden building also has a garden and a quay on the lake.

10 VENTISQUERO NEGRO ✱✱✱
The snout of the Manso glacier is a cliff face of ice and sediment lying in a valley.

6 CAMPING LOS RAPIDOS ✱✱

INSCRIPTIONS

▬▬	Asphalt Road
═══	Gravel Road
·······	Graded Earth Road
123	National Route
123	Provincial Route
─·─	International Border

11 LOS VENTISQUEROS HOTEL ✱✱

THE LOS CESARES ROUTE
The Los Cesares river flows from a waterfall by Hotel Tronador into the lake of the same name. You can reach them by a footpath that starts near the hotel.

12 MONTE TRONADOR ✱✱✱ *At 3,478 m (11,410 ft) in height, it is the highest peak in Nahuel Huapi national Park, and is very popular with mountaineers.*

SIGHTS TO SEE

- LAKE MASCARDI
- MIRADOR SOBRE ISLA CORAZON
- VENTISQUERO NEGRO
- MONTE TRONADOR

FACTS

DENSE FOREST
This route runs through a high, dense forest that contains typical trees of the area like maitén and cypress.

9 PAMPA LINDA ✱✱✱
20 km of grassy mudflats, hotels and camping areas.

4 MANSO RIVER ✱✱✱
Flows from the southern end of Lake Mascardi to Lake Hess, further west. We recommend its rapids (great for whitewater rafting) and the nearby Los Alerces waterfall.

7 MIRADOR SOBRE ISLA CORAZON ✱✱✱
One of the best views of Lake Mascardi.

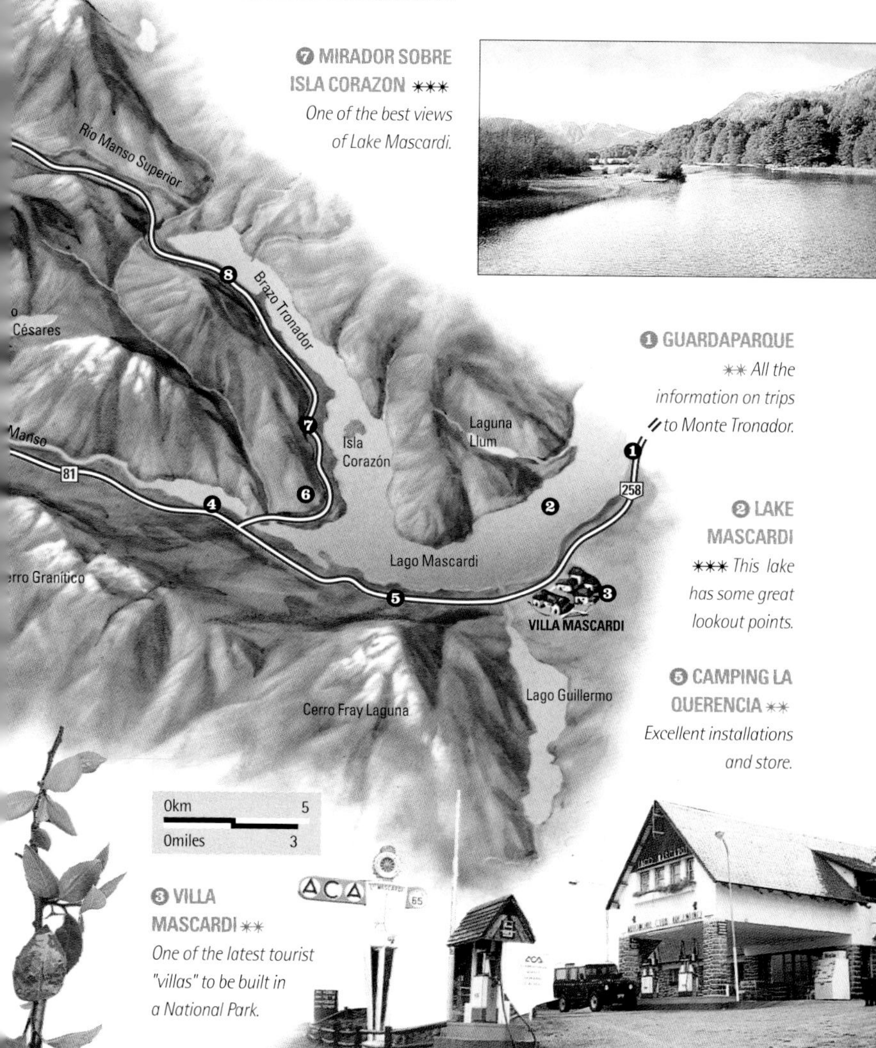

1 GUARDAPARQUE ✱✱ *All the information on trips to Monte Tronador.*

2 LAKE MASCARDI ✱✱✱ *This lake has some great lookout points.*

5 CAMPING LA QUERENCIA ✱✱
Excellent installations and store.

3 VILLA MASCARDI ✱✱
One of the latest tourist "villas" to be built in a National Park.

This up-and-down route (gravel path, then the RN 258) runs along Lake Gutiérrez and passes Villa Arelauquén, lookout points, hotels, teahouses and woodland. After Gutiérrez, grassy mudflats with a just-visible watershed lead on to the Park Warden's Post.

BOAT TRIP

Visitors can also get to Monte Tronador on the motorboat Victoria II, *which sails from Villa Mascardí and can carry 150 passengers. The boat arrives at Hotel Tronador, from where a bus takes you up to the mountain.*

GUARDAPARQUE 1

The Park Warden's Post. Check here on the state of the routes and the Monte Tronador ascent and descent schedules (the path is one-way). There are also schedule restrictions on the outbound path to Los Alerces waterfall.

▶ *The Park Warden's post is located above the eastern end of Lake Mascardí; the route runs along the south shore.*

LAKE MASCARDI 2

The shore of Lake Mascardi.

Like most lakes in this area, Mascardí is glacial. It is V-shaped, and the Tronador stretch is the most attractive of the two. Nearby woodland includes coigues, lengas, cypresses, ñires and maitenes. Mascardí is ideal for sports fishing, and the Upper Manso river flows into it on the west side. This river, which flows down from Mt. Tronador's glaciers, is the main tributary. The River Fresco exits from the lake's east side, while water from Lake Guillermo flows into it on the southeast side.

▶ *After passing a wood 3 km from Mascardí, we reach the first of three lookout points over the lake. 2 km further on, the path reaches Villa Mascardí.*

VILLA MASCARDI 3

Built in Nahuel Huapi national park (which explains its slow, uneven growth), this is one of the most recent tourist "villas". It includes two hotels ,the Hotel Lago Mascardí and the Hotel de Gas del Estado. There also number of private houses with lovely gardens, as well as several service buildings.

Service station at Villa Mascardí.

▶ *Take the RN 258. After the bridge, the RP 81 (on the left) leads to the southern end of the lake, which connects with the Manso River, on the west side.*

THE MANSO RIVER 4

The Manso River actually begins 8 km further on, where the Tron-

The fast-flowing Manso River is ideal for whitewater rafting.

ador stretch of Lake Mascardí curves towards Gutiérrez. In spite of its name (Manso means gentle), it is a fast-flowing river filled with rapids, ideal for rafting and fishing, especially fly fishing. When you reach the bridge that runs over it – 8 km after taking the RP 81 – the road splits into two. One path follows the coast of Mascardí, while the other leads first to Lake Hess, then on to Lake Fonck.

► *The park's curving entrance path leads down through woodland featuring cypresses, coigue and maitén. La Querencia stands at the point where the bridge crosses the Yocondo river.*

LA QUERENCIA CAMSITE 5

The La Querencia campsite.

Campsite.This campsite has all the installations you'll need, including a well-stocked store (one of the few in the area). The site, which is very popular with students, was created by one of the first Swiss families that settled in this area. Campers can also go horse-riding.

► *After the Yocondo river, 2 km (1,2 miles) of flatter land leads to another bridge over the Manso River. Cross this, and on your right is the route to the Camping Los Rápidos.*

Lake Mascardí (with Isla Corazon in the background) tends to vary in color.

LAKE GUILLELMO

After passing Villa Mascardí, continue along the RN 258 as far as Guillelmo. It has a number of quiet spots for camping amongst maitén, cypresses and broom.

CAMPING LOS RAPIDOS 6

Campsite.This is an ideal place to stop for a snack, or you may choose to spend the day on the lake. Visitors can hire kayaks and fishing equipment. A very popular fishing place.

► *Take the path along the Tronador stretch, between tall, thick coigue woods. 7 km from Los Rápidos you reach the lookout point over isla Corazon.*

LOOKOUT POINT OVER ISLA CORAZON 7

A natural balcony over the Tronador stretch of lake Mascardí. Notice how the gradually-changing light transforms the lake and mountain landscape, and admire the coigue and cypress woods by the side of the lake, with isla Corazon in the middle. The water varies in color, and is milky-whitish where the Manso flows into it.

A BEAUTIFUL WATERFALL

Before taking the bridge over the Manso River, there is a path on the left which leads to this waterfall. The water drops 20 m (65 ft.) down past mossy walls into the Manso River's deep pools.

A steep stretch of path leads into a tall, leafy wood. The gradient then levels out, the path narrows and you pass a turnoff to the Pío XI cabin (15 minutes away). 7 km (4 miles) from the lookout point over Isla Corazon you see the entrance to Hotel Tronador on the right.

HOTEL TRONADOR 8

Hotel Tronador stands at the north end of Lake Mascardí's Tronador stretch – almost at the lake's end. Built in 1929 by the Vereertbrugghen family (of Belgian origin), it is surrounded by high peaks such as Cerro Bonete, and has an excellent view of the Tronador massif. It is comprised of three log buildings and is surrounded by a lovely garden. Visitors can enjoy home cooking, day trips, fishing, canoeing, horse-riding and walks.

INFORMATION: TEL (02944) 46-8127.

▶ *Near the hotel there is an optional path to the Los Césares waterfall. After 2 km (1.2 miles), Lake Mascardí ends and the path descends to the Upper Manso River valley and Pampa Linda - 22 km (13.5 miles) of lookout points, grassland and a campsite after the bridge over the Manso.*

THE KING OF PATAGONIA

A French adventurer called Orelie-Antoine de Tounens arrived in Chile in 1858, and in 1860 proclaimed himself King of Independent Araucania. His "kingdom" included South Chile and Patagonia. "Dethroned" in 1871, he returned to France. Died in 1878.

PAMPA LINDA 9

Campsite in Pampa Linda.

The Pampa Linda is an area of extensive grassy mudflats – a flatter, more open landscape than the dense woodland through which this route passes. The Manso River flows along to the right of the path, which runs through bushes such as the abundant culeu. Visitors wishing to stop here can stay in the Hostería Pampa Linda, established in 1940 by Benito Vereertbrugghen. Next door there is a 40-room hotel, a park warden's post and a well-equipped campsite affiliated to the Bariloche Mountaineer's Club.

▶ *After 1 km (0.5 miles), there is a turnoff on the left to the lovely Las Nalcas waterfall (20 minutes). Go through a wood of ñires and lengas, and the path enters another wood of taller trees. 8 km (5 miles) further on, after a steep climb, lies Nahuel Huapi.*

VENTISQUERO NEGRO 10

A black icefield. Also known as the Manso icefield, as it is the snout of the Manso glacier. It consists of huge brownish-gray ice blocks created by avalanches of ice, mud and boulders, and which were then dragged along by the advancing glacier. The glacier starts at the upper ice cap on Mt. Tronador. As it moves downhill, it creates ice showers which are more dramatic in summer and in the evenings. The rumbling noise that comes from Mt. Tronador is caused by the

The icefield's dark color comes from the sediment in the Manso glacier.

clashing of ice blocks. The Manso River is fed by glacial meltwater which flows down and eventually out into the Pacific.

► *The steep climb continues along a number of curving dirt paths. After approx. 2 km (1 mile) the vehicle route ends at Hostería Los Ventisqueros.*

HOSTERIA LOS VENTISQUEROS 11

The hostel is at the foot of Mt. Tronador.

The hostel has a large parking area and extensive leisure facilities – baths, bar and restaurant service. A good place to rest and wait until the descent path for the Mt. Tronador route opens in the afternoon. Walkers can rest in the shade of lenga trees. A 30-minute footpath leads to the waterfalls on the eastern cliffs of Mt. Tronador.

The Mt. Tronador massif - very popular with mountain climbers.

THE HIGH PEAKS

8 km (5 miles) along Pampa Linda valley there is a lookout point with a view of Mt. Tronador and other peaks. There is an identification sign showing their silhouettes, names and respective heights.

► *Walkers can reach the glacier's snout by different paths. To reach the eastern cliffs of Mt. Tronador, leave your vehicle and take a 30-minute footpath.*

MONTE TRONADOR 12

This is the highest mountain in Nahuel Huapi national park, and is permanently capped with ice. It has three peaks: the Chilean one, the Argentine one and an international one. On the north-east side stands the Meiling refuge, which is the main shelter for climbers scaling this mountain. It can be reached along a path that starts after Pampa Linda. Use the same path for the return journey. ■

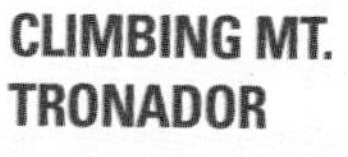

CLIMBING MT. TRONADOR

The route up to the peaks begins at the Meiling refuge (2,050 meters - 6,725 ft.). With its icy, snowy surface and the constant danger of avalanches, this is a route only for experienced climbers.

A Big Green Nature Reserve

Andean valleys with tiny villages filled with history and tradition, and offering all kinds of excursions to mountains, lakes and fast-flowing rivers. The area between Río Negro and Río Chubut is virtually virgin land, packed with unique flora and fauna.

LAKE VERDE

CARVED FOREST

EL BOLSON

LAKE PUELO

TREVELIN

ANDEAN REGION ON THE 42ND PARALLEL

COUNTRY MARKET IN EL BOLSON

ITINERARY 5

WATERFALL AT LAKE CISNE

LAKE RIVADAVIA

MAITEN

WELSH COAT OF ARMS

LA TROCHITA TRAIN AT ESQUEL

PARQUE NACIONAL LAGO PUELO

El Bolsón to Trevelín

This route runs through the provinces of Rio Negro and Chubut, which contain some of the largest, least-exploited natural spaces in Andean Patagonia. Sector 1 route explores the area around El Bolsón – a mountain village in a valley with easy access to excellent excursions. Sector 2 route takes in the lakes and rivers of the enormous Los Alerces national park, the largest in the area, plus the towns of Esquel and Trevelín, which are of great historical interest.

Sector 1
EL BOLSON TO LAKE PUELO

SIGHTS TO SEE

❶ El Bolsón ✱✱✱✱ ❷ Cerro Piltriquitrón ✱✱✱ ❸ Bosque Tallado ✱✱✱ ❹ Cerro Perito Moreno ✱✱ ❺ The Mallín Ahogado circular route ✱✱✱ ❻ Parque Nacional LagoPuelo ✱✱✱✱

SOME TIPS

There are lots of recommendable excursions in the area around El Bolsón. Stay a few days in the area and enjoy them all.

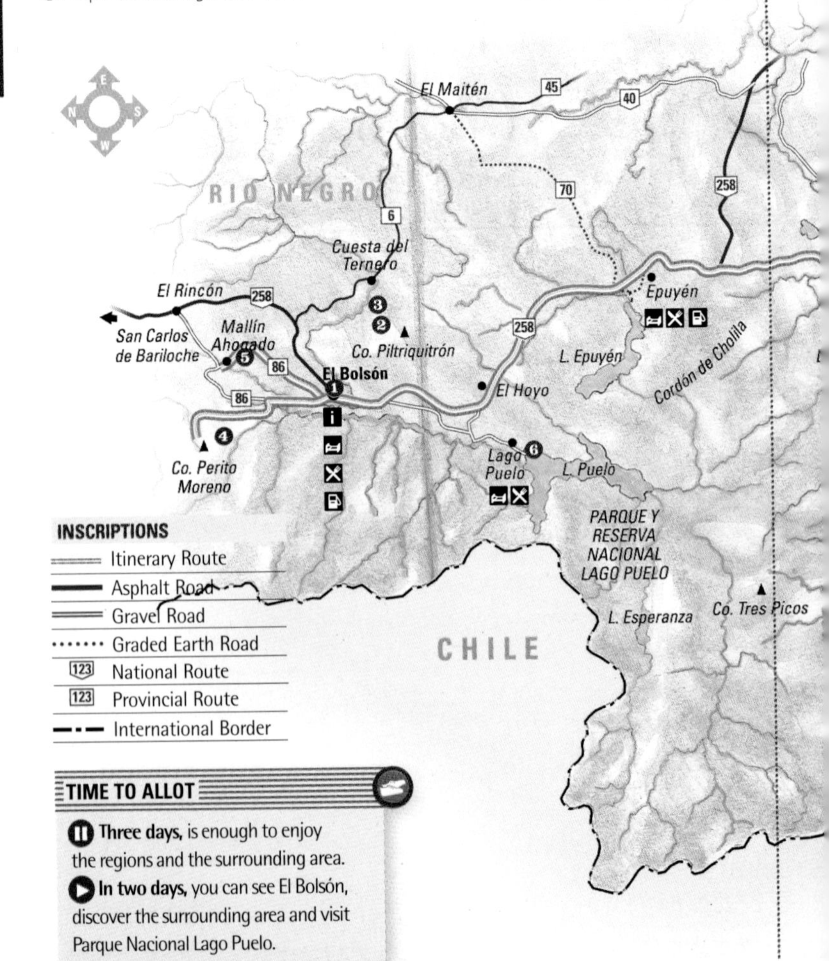

TIME TO ALLOT

Three days, is enough to enjoy the regions and the surrounding area.

In two days, you can see El Bolsón, discover the surrounding area and visit Parque Nacional Lago Puelo.

TIME TO ALLOT	II	Detailed visit: seven days.
	▶	Rapid visit: five days.
DISTANCE	KM	Approx. 225 km. (140 mi.)
MEANS		By car.

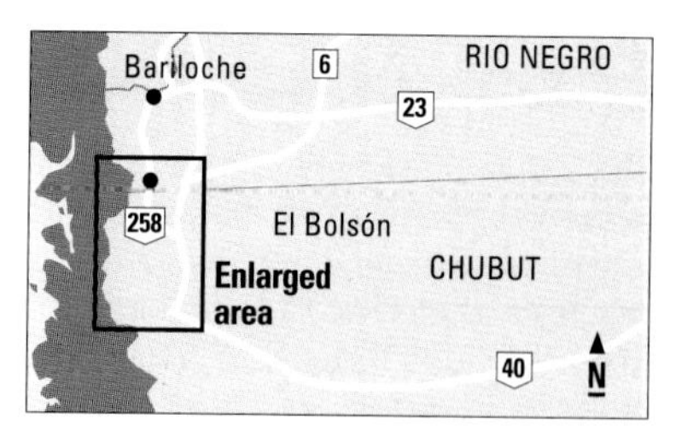

Sector 2
CHOLILA TO TREVELIN

SIGHTS TO SEE

❶ Cholila ✳ ❷ Parque Nacional Los Alerces ✳✳✳✳ L. Rivadavia, Lake Verde, Arrayanes River, L. Menéndez, L. Futalaufquen, Villa Futalaufquen, Percey Valley ❸ Esquel ✳✳✳ ❹ Trevelín ✳✳ ❺ Futalaufú Dam ✳✳

TIME TO ALLOT

II **Four days** minimum if you want to explore this large area thoroughly.
▶ **In three days** you can spend one day in Los Alerces, sleep at Esquel or travel the next day, stop in at Trevelín and even see the dam on day 3.

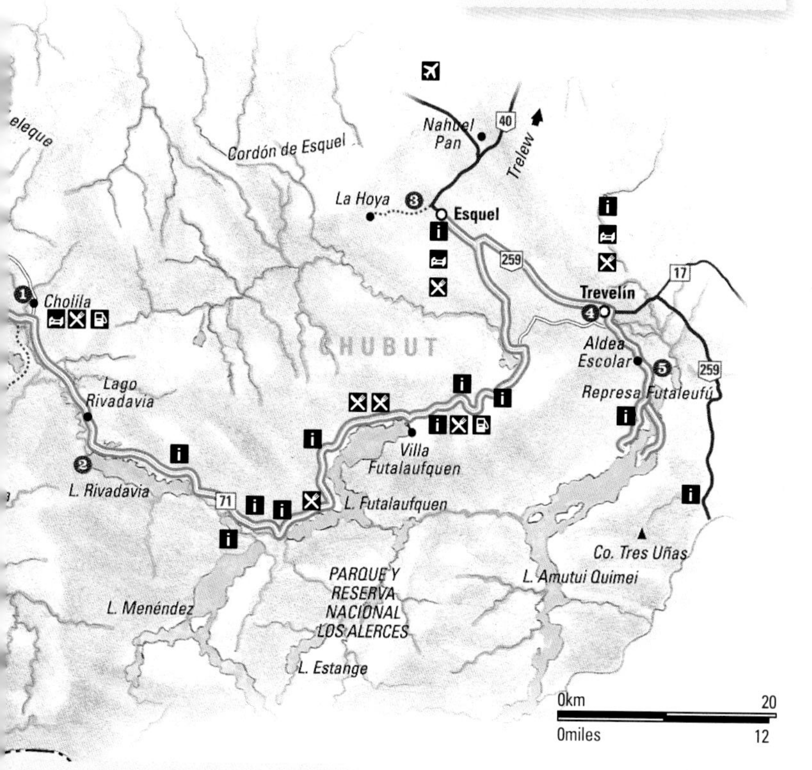

SOME TIPS

You might come across a rock fall on the gravel road that crosses Los Alerces national park. Be sure to check on the state of the path before you start your journey.

REFERENCES

- INFORMATION PAGE 128 - BASIC DATA
- SERVICE STATION PAGE 130 - TRANSPORTATION
- AIRPORT PAGE 131 - TRANSPORTATION
- HOTEL PAGE 132 - ACCOMMODATION
- RESTAURANT PAGE 136 - RESTAURANT

El Bolsón to Lake Puelo

The fertile Andean region of parallel 42 is the hub of this route. The picturesque town of El Bolsón is located in a valley with lots of possible excursions. To the south, lake Puelo lies in the park of the same name.

❻ PARQUE NACIONAL LAGO PUELO ✱✱✱✱

23,700 hectares in size (9,480 acres), the park features mountains and glacial valleys, as well as Lake Puelo and a totally unique flora.

THINKING GREEN

El Bolsón was declared an ecologically-friendly municipality in 1991.

0km 20
0miles 12

LAGO PUELO
❻
258
Lago Puelo
Lago Epuyén
Cordón de Cholila

INSCRIPTIONS

- Asphalt Road
- Gravel Road
- Graded Earth Road
- 123 National Route
- 123 Provincial Route

❹ CERRO PERITO MORENO ✱✱

The site of the eponymous ski center.

SIGHTS TO SEE

- EL BOLSON
- BOSQUE TALLADO
- MALLIN AHOGADO CIRCULAR ROUTE
- PARQUE NACIONAL LAGO PUELO

FACTS

HIDDEN WATERS
Near Mallín Ahogado waterfall lies the Escondida ("Hidden") waterfall and the outstanding Botanic Gardens.

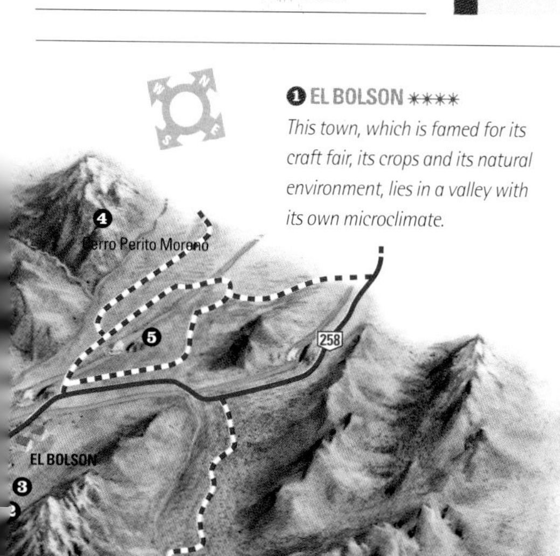

❶ EL BOLSON ✱✱✱✱

This town, which is famed for its craft fair, its crops and its natural environment, lies in a valley with its own microclimate.

❷ CERRO PILTRIQUITRON ✱✱✱

This huge block of stone stands beside El Bolsón. A mountain path goes up one side to a lookout point with an excellent view of the valley.

❸ BOSQUE TALLADO

✱✱✱ *A permanent outdoor exhibition of statues carved into the trunks of burnt trees.*

❺ MALLIN AHOGADO CIRCULAR ROUTE ✱✱✱

Just a few kilometers from El Bolsón, this route includes the two waterfalls and the beautiful Botanic Gardens.

This route begins at El Bolsón, in the Andean region of parallel 42, between Rio Negro and Chubut provinces. Take the (asphalt road) RN 258 to drive there from the north.

El Bolsón stands by the Quemquemtreu River and at the foot of Cerro Piltriquitrón.

EL BOLSON 1

This picturesque town stands on the edge of the Quemquemtreu River, in the fertile Valle Nuevo. It is surrounded by the Loma del Medio mountains and the Piltriquitrón chain. The houses are mostly stone, with cypress-wood tiled roofs. The valley's microclimate and average height make it perfect for agriculture. The main crops are strawberries, raspberries, cherries, malt, redcurrants, elder and sweet brier. The local people live in harmony with nature, and their way of life gives the area its particular flavor.

► *Take the RN 258 out of El Bolsón. When you get to Villa Turismo, there is a rough gravel road that leads up to Piltriquitrón (30 minutes by car), with a lookout point after 13 km (9 miles).*

CERRO PILTRIQUITRON 2

Cerro Piltriquitrón, a great lookout point.

Piltriquitrón is 2,260 m high (7,414 ft.). A path winds its way more than 1,000 m (3,280 ft.) up the mountainside to a platform with a view of El Bolsón. On clear days you can see Mt. Tronador and the glaciers behind Lake Puelo.

► *At the end of the Piltriquitrón path there is a signpost to the Carved Forest sculptures (a steep 40-minute climb).*

BOSQUE TALLADO 3

The Carved Forest. In a woodland clearing created by a fire, artists such as Nadia Guthmann, Enrique Aros, Susanna Vallone, Juan C. Toledo, Raphael Roca and others made sculptures out of burned-out tree trunks.

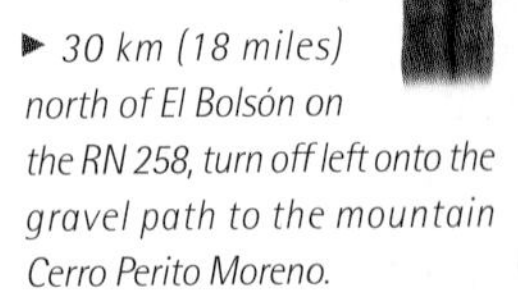

► *30 km (18 miles) north of El Bolsón on the RN 258, turn off left onto the gravel path to the mountain Cerro Perito Moreno.*

HANDICRAFTS IN EL BOLSON

El Bolsón Craft Fair is open on Mondays, Thursdays and Saturdays from 10:00 - 14:00 hours. It started in 1979, and now has over 50 handcrafted items on sale. Well-known for their quality and originality, these are sold in fairs throughout the country.

CERRO PERITO MORENO 4

This mountain has the La Comarca ski center mountain shelter. A three-hour walk from this spot across a high plain leads to a glacier at the summit.

▶ *Take the northbound RN 258 out of El Bolsón. Turn right at the crossing and in 10 km (6.2 miles) you reach the Mallín Ahogado circular route, which has several places of interest.*

MALLIN AHOGADO CIRCULAR ROUTE 5

The Mallín Ahogado waterfall.

After a slope up through pine trees, a turnoff leads to the "Hidden" waterfall and the Botanic Gardens on the left, while on the right there is the Mallín Ahogado waterfall, over 20 meters high.

DISCOVERING THE 42nd PARALLEL

El Bolsón is an excellent base for taking trips into the surrounding area.
The best of these trips include Cerro Lindo (two days, on foot or on horseback), Cajón Azul (where you can try all kinds of natural products) and El Hoyo waterfall, where you can reach out and touch the falling water. Also worth a trip: the Virgen Misionera waterfall, La Lorna del Medio and the Azul River.

▶ *Avenida San Martín in El Bolsón crosses the 42nd parallel and connects with the right turnoff to the town of Lake Puelo (9 km /5,5 miles). After 18 km (11 miles) you reach the Lake Puelo national Park. La Playita lakeshore beach is not far from here.*

PARQUE NACIONAL LAGO PUELO 6

Located between glacial valleys and mountains, this park was created in 1937 and stretches over 23,700 hectares (9,480 acres). 200 m (656 ft.) above sea level, its microclimate is home to a flora that is totally unique in Argentina. Apart from the beaches of fine sand and lakeside camping areas, there are also several roads, footpaths and boat trips to enjoy. The hotels, campsite, store, cafe and restaurant will all make you want to stay longer. ■

III INFORMATION: TEL. (02944) 49-9064.

Lake Puelo, in the national park of the same name.

LAKE EPUYEN

Go south (RN 258) out of El Bolsón. After 15 km (9 miles) there's a turnoff to El Hoyo, famous for its fruit. Lake Epuyen turnoff (beach and campsite) comes after 37 km.

Cholila to Trevelín

One of the most spectacular routes in this book runs through a huge basin of lakes, woods and rivers north of Chubut province, and which is now a national park. At the other end, across the Patagonian steppes, lie the towns of Esquel and Trevelín, which are rich in history, and a large hydroelectric power plant.

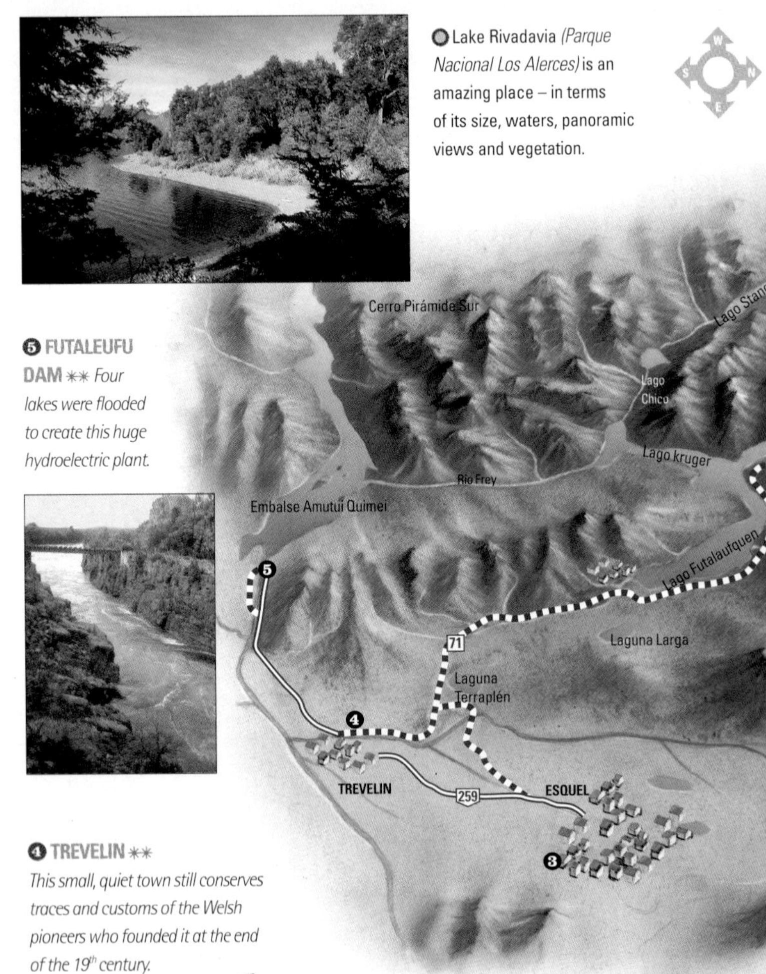

Lake Rivadavia *(Parque Nacional Los Alerces)* is an amazing place – in terms of its size, waters, panoramic views and vegetation.

5 FUTALEUFU DAM ✱✱ *Four lakes were flooded to create this huge hydroelectric plant.*

4 TREVELIN ✱✱ *This small, quiet town still conserves traces and customs of the Welsh pioneers who founded it at the end of the 19th century.*

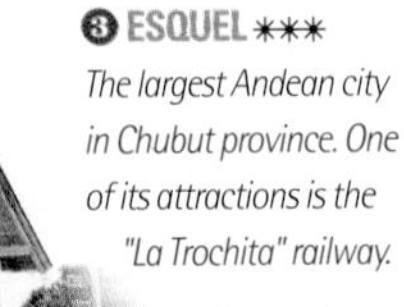

3 ESQUEL ✱✱✱ *The largest Andean city in Chubut province. One of its attractions is the "La Trochita" railway.*

SIGHTS TO SEE

- PARQUE NACIONAL LOS ALERCES
- ESQUEL
- TREVELIN
- FUTALEUFU DAM

FACTS

THE LELEQUE MUSEUM
This museum of archeology and Patagonian history is based in a ranch belonging to the Benetton group in Leleque.

INSCRIPTIONS

- Asphalt Road
- Gravel Road
- Graded Earth Road
- 123 National Route
- 123 Provincial Route

The Arrayanes river *(Parque Nacional Los Alerces)* is crystal-clear and navigable. Also has a number of beaches.

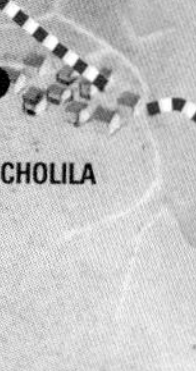

2 PARQUE NACIONAL LOS ALERCES ****

Places of interest:

- Lake Rivadavia
- Lake Verde
- River Arrayanes
- Lake Menéndez
- Lake Futalaufquén
- Villa Futalaufquen
- Percey River Valley

Lake Futalaufquén *(Parque Nacional Los Alerces).*

Bust of Perito Moreno at Villa Futalaufquén *(Parque Nacional Los Alerces).*

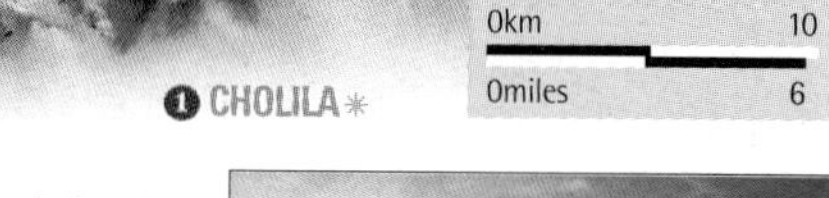

1 CHOLILA *

Lake Menéndez *(P. N. Los Alerces)*, the largest lake in the park, has three main channels, as well as a small island and a thousand year-old forest in the north.

This itinerary starts south of El Bolsón, on the RN 258. After 50 km (31 miles), a left turnoff (RP 71 – gravel road) leads to the town of Cholila, 40 km (25 miles) further on.

CHOLILA 1

In the Mapuche language, Cholila means "beautiful valley". The town, located between four valleys, was colonized at the end of the 19th-century by descendants of European and Syrian-Lebanese immigrants. It has hotels and good food for visitors keen on mountain climbing, hunting on fishing (in Lake Cholila, 2 km [1.2 miles] from here).

LAND OF GLACIERS
This area includes fea-tures from the Quaternary period, when it was completely iced-over. The channels of Lake Menendez are the result of glacial action.

▶ *Get back onto the RP 71, and go on along the Los Castillos mountain chain. After 20 Km (12 miles), a road makes the climb to the park entrance.*

BUTCH CASSIDY'S CABIN

At the beginning of the 20th century, three Americans settled in a house near Cholila and began cattle-raising. They left in 1905, and later it was discovered that two of them were the legendary outlaws Butch Cassidy and the Sundance Kid.

PARQUE NACIONAL LOS ALERCES 2

This park was created in 1937, to conserve the thousand-year-old larch forests, as the larch is a long-living species that is very difficult to reforest. The park is enormous (187,500 hectares of national park and 75,000 hectares of nature reserve) and is comprised of a complex system of lakes that flow into the Futaleufú river, which in turn flows into the Pacific. The landscape includes wooded mountains and peaks such as Cordón de las Pirámides, Cerro Torrecillas and Cordón Situación.

MORE INFORMATION ON PP. 122-123.

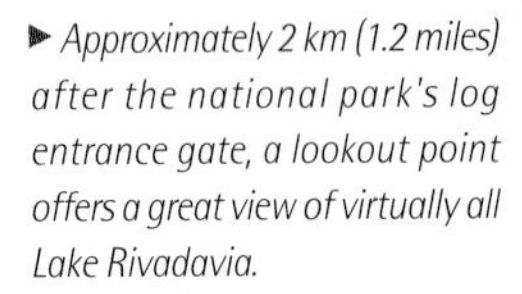

▶ *Approximately 2 km (1.2 miles) after the national park's log entrance gate, a lookout point offers a great view of virtually all Lake Rivadavia.*

LAKE RIVADAVIA 1

Sandy beach at Lake Rivadavia.

The area around lake Rivadavia, which can be seen clearly from the cliff paths, are covered with mixed woodland – cypress, broom and elder trees. The route has several lookout points, park wardens' posts and access to well-equipped campsites.

▶ *Park warden's post after 3 km. Follow the Rivadavia river; there's a lookout point after a bridge and an 8-km (5-mile) climb to Lake Verde lookout point.*

The Arrayanes River, which runs through Parque Nacional Los Alerces.

LAKE VERDE ②

This lookout point has a splendid view of a huge forest, plus Lake Menéndez and the Arrayanes river. There is a campsite on the shore of tiny Lake Verde (called thus because of its deep green color). 2 km (1. miles) from the lookout point, a 1-km (0.5-mile) path crosses a footbridge and leads to Puerto Chucao, on Lake Menéndez.

Lake Verde in winter.

▶ *After the Lake Verde lookout point and passing the turnoff to Puerto Chucao (and the boat trip), you see the Arrayanes park warden's post. Another 2 km (1 mile) and you reach the lookout point above the Arrayanes river.*

THE ARRAYANES RIVER 

This river runs through a valley lined with woodland. Water volume drops significantly in summer, making boat use impossible. A hanging footbridge over the river provides access to Puerto Chucao, where you can take a boat trip on Lake Menéndez. This is the only boat trip available in the drier summer season.

One of Lake Menéndez' three channels, with thick woodland on the shore.

Hanging bridge over the Arrayanes river

▶ *Routes around Lake Menéndez start from the other side of the Arrayanes river, by the footbridge.*

LAKE MENENDEZ 

Lake Menéndez is the largest of the park's natural lakes - though Amutui Quimei (on the south side of the national park) is larger, it is a man-made dam, built in the 1970s. Lake Menéndez has three channels as well as Isla Grande. Boat trips around the lake leave from Puerto Chucao, sailing as far as the north channel and the thousand-year-old larch forests on Lake Cisne. The mountainsides east and west of Menéndez are covered with coigue and cypress trees, with larches on the north and south sides.

THOUSAND-YEAR-OLD GIANTS

A boat trip takes you to the north channel of Lake Menéndez and the Puerto Sagrario thousand-year-old larch forest. It has larches 2,000 to 3,000 years old; some are over 50 m (164 ft.) high, and 4 m (13 ft.) in diameter.

Go along the Arrayanes river, which has a campsite on its banks. Soon the river widens at the north end of Lake Futalaufquen.

LAKE FUTALAUFQUEN 5

Lying amidst lush vegetation and backed by snowy peaks, Futalaufquen has lots of lookout points, beaches (i.e. the Francés) fishermen's hostels, a port, log cabins, stores, campsites and free camping areas. There is a 30-km (18.5-mile) path along the eastern lakeshore.

In the distance – the southern shore of Futalaufquen.

► *At the end of the route around Lake Futalaufquen, an asphalt path leads up to Villa Futalaufquen, near the Los Alerces national park headquarters.*

The Percey river valley, an example of a pre-glacial valley.

HANGING GLACIER
In the northeast of the park stands Cerro Torrecillas, nearby a hanging glacier with a drop of 300m (984 ft.). Very popular with mountain climbers.

VILLA FUTALAUFQUEN 6

This tourist Villa was built near the Los Alerces national park headquarters, a log building on a hill. This small, low-rise town provides accommodation for the national park staff and has a number of stores. The park exit is near the Villa.

► *A curved, rising path is followed by a descent down a glacial moraine. Take the bridge over the narrow river, and from here there is a view of the Percey river valley.*

PERCY RIVER VALLEY 7

The somewhat chaotic appearance of the valleys in this area (i.e. the Percey valley, named for one of the welsh pioneers who arrived at the end of the 19th century) was caused by glacial action. However, the Percy valley is pre-glacial, dating back to the Quaternary period. After a steep descent with sharp bends you see cypress and maitén trees on the grassy mud flats and the Terraplén lagoon.

LA TROCHITA

The Old Patagonian Express (or Narrow Gauge Train) was built in Belgium and the United States in the 1920s. It travels the line between Esquel and El Maitén on rails with a gauge of 75 cm (29 inches). Take it to Nahuel Pan (2 hours), with a trip to see Mapuche craftsmen included.

► *Turn left from the gravel path onto the asphalt RN 259; after a gentle upward slope of 10 km (6 miles) you reach Esquel.*

ESQUEL 3

Lookout point with view of Esquel.

Located in a valley between two hills, this is the largest city in the Andean province of Chubut, and has 20,000 inhabitants. It was officially founded on February 25th 1906 by Welsh colonists, though it had already been in existence for two years. Nearby attractions include La Hoya ski center and the historic railway line La Trochita. Esquel has an excellent tourist infrastructure and is ideal as a base for taking trips to nearby areas (Los Alerces and Trevelín, for example).

THE WELSH OF THE SOUTH

An old mill in Trevelín contains (as well as some public organizations) the Museum of Wales, which has shields, documents, furniture, clothing and an organ, all brought by the first of the Welsh colonists.

Museo Galés (Museum of Wales). 9 AM - 9 PM (high season) and 11 AM - 7:30 PM (low season).

► *Leave Esquel by the same route (RN 259). After 24 km (15 miles) of asphalt road, you reach Trevelín.*

TREVELIN 4

Welsh, Trevelín means "mill town". Most of its 5,000 inhabitants descended from the Welsh colonists who arrived in 1902. They have kept alive their ancestors' language and customs, such as tea drinking, welsh cakes and Eisteddfod, a competition of poetry, music and dance, which has a typical Welsh armchair as a prize. 15 km (9 miles) from this cattle-farming town lies the Nant y Fall waterfall ("falling stream" in Welsh"), which is actually three waterfalls, with a drop of 60 m (196 ft.). Also has a camping area.

► *20 km (12 miles) from Trevelín, surfaced and gravel roads take you to Futaleufú dam, which you reach 10 km (6 miles) further on.*

THE FUTALEUFU DAM 5

The reservoir at the Futaleufú complex.

This huge hydroelectric plant was built between 1973 and 1978 on the source of the Futaleufú river, on the southern side of the Los Alerces national park. To carry out this huge project, a number of lakes in the area were flooded to create a huge man-made reservoir, with a dam wall 120 m (328 ft.) high. Organized tours allowed. ■

•› MORE INFORMATION ON PP. 124-125.

The old mill – Los Andes de Trevelín – is now home to the Museum of Wales.

Parque Nacional Los Alerces

A larch forest. Created in 1937 and almost 263,000 hectares in size, this natural system of lakes, rivers and reservoir amazes visitors with its size, lookout points, crystal-clear water and lush flora. The park's emblem is the huge larch (alarce), one of the longest-living tree species in the world.

THE GRAVEL ROAD that winds through the foothills of the mountains provides views of the rivers and lakes of Los Alerces, like this panoramic view of Lake Verde.

BOAT TRIPS *through the park's lakes and rivers leave from different quays such as Puerto Limonao.*

THREE HOSTELS, *several campsites, cabins and settlers houses can be found by the lakes and rivers.*

THE BANDURRIA IBIS, *the condor and the Araucana dove all inhabit in this ecosystem.*

THE LAKE SYSTEM which makes up the park's hydrography includes species of flora such as the Amancay.

THE ENTRANCE *to the park from the Futulaufquen lakeshore.*

USEFUL INFORMATION

ADDRESS: To get to Los Alerces National Park, drive 67 km (41.5 miles) along the RP 71 from Esquel, Trevelin or Cholila. The information office is at Villa Futulaufquen: tel: (02945) 47 - 1015/10200.

VISITS: There is no park access schedule, though visitors entering after 8 A.M. must pay an entrance fee.

FACTS

FOR BACKPACKERS

There are 100 km (62 miles) of beautiful footpaths running through the park to locations such as this one: Siete Saltos.

THE LAKE BASIN in which this park lies used to have 17 lakes, but lost four of them to the reservoir. One of them was the Futulaufquen – 7,000 hectares in size and with an average depth of 150 m (492 ft.).

WIDE SANDY BEACHES *abound on the park's lakeshores and riverbanks, with camping areas and quays nearby.*

FLORA. *Larches, radals, ipomeas and other trees and shrubs add a touch of green to the area.*

1,000-YEAR-OLD LARCH FOREST. The wettest areas of the National Park are home to the tree that gives it its name. This conifer grows very in damp ground, and the longest-living ones only have branches at the top. The park's most famous larch wood is Puerto Sagrario, north of Lake Menéndez.

Puerto Sagrario larch forest.

EVERLASTING TREES . *The larch grows 1 mm in diameter a year. Larches 3,600 years old have been recorded, though one tree here – "The Grandfather" is around 2,600 years old.*

Water Power

The Patagonian lake corridor's huge water resources, following construction of the Futaleufú dam in the Los Alerces lake basin, have been harnessed to create electrical energy. Situated beside an artificial lake, this is the largest hydroelectric plant in the region.

The dam

◀ Built in the 1970s, the Futaleufú hydroelectric plant stretches over 100 hectares and produces energy for the Aluar aluminum plant in Puerto Madryn. 6,000 workers were involved in building the complex.

6,000

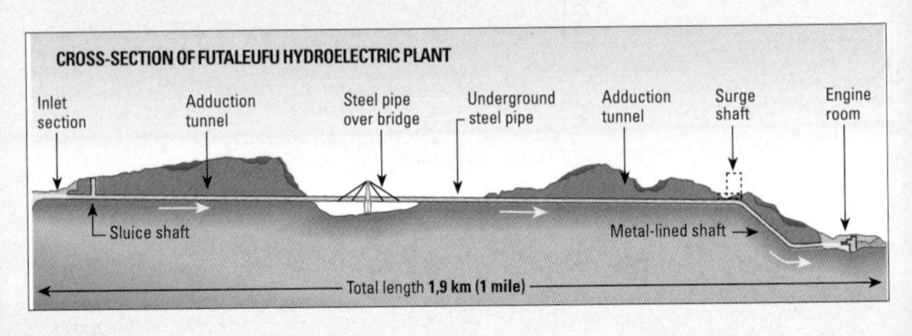

Tank

◀ The dam's surge shaft is 62 m (203 ft.) high and 28 m (91 ft.) in diameter. An inverted interior cone regulates the flow of water through 1,895 m (6,217 ft.) of tunnels.

▲ **ENERGY.** Futaleufú *(photo: the course of the dry dock)* has 448 MW of power and produces an average of 2,600 GW per hour.

A MASSIVE RESERVOIR
Four of Los Alerces national park's lakes disappeared intothe dam's artificial lake, Amutui Quimei. A total average of 300,000 liters (79,260 gallons) per second of water flow through the park.

Flow

▶ Two bridges were built over the Futaleufú river (on the source of which the dam stands) between 1970 and 1978. It flows into the Rio Grande, which in turn flows out into the Pacific. The Futaleufú has a maximum water flow of 5,300m³ (17,388 ft³) per second, with an average of 292m³ (957 ft³) per second.

5,300

▶ **13 INTERCONNECTED LAKES** flow into the Futaleufú river and on into Lake Yelcho *(photo: Yrigoyen waterfall, at Futalauquén).*

▼ **STEEL PIPES** over bridges and underground transport water from the reservoir at a rate of up to 360m³ per second.

Vineyards

Another artificial water system was built in Rio Negro Valley in the 1920s, to generate energy and irrigate vineyards and apple orchards.

THE ARRIVAL OF WATER *in the upper Rio Negro valley (photo above: a canning factory) led to a boom in fruit production and attracted many immigrants.*

THE BALLESTER LEVELING DAM in 1910, built in the upper Rio Negro valley.

LAS BALSAS HOTEL IN VILLA LA ANGOSTURA

CANOEING ON THE LAKES

THE ROUTE TO CERRO CATEDRAL

PARAGLIDING OVER LAKE NAHUEL HUAPI

MAPUCHE PITCHER

LOG CABINS IN SAN MARTIN DE LOS ANDES

LOOKOUT POINT AT PARQUE NACIONAL LOS ALERCES

BAR IN CERRO CHAPELCO

PHONE BOOTH

CATAMARAN AT PUERTO QUETRIHUE

CABLE CARS TO CERRO CHAPELCO

RAFTING

SERVICES

Useful Data

This section contains all the information you need to enjoy yourself in Southern Patagonia: telephone numbers, directions, transport services for traveling around this vast region, hotels, log cabins and other accommodation, as well as the best places for local cuisine, all the sports and leisure activities that are available in the mountains, lakes and forests, and all the typical local products you can take home as souvenirs.

SUMMARY

MENU SELECTION

SKIER

SWIMMING POOL AT HOTEL LLAO LLAO

ICE SKATING IN BARILOCHE

Practical Information

There is so much to see in the lakes region that we suggest visitors plan their trip carefully. Bear in mind that tourist numbers depend on the weather, and check out the park regulations, festivals and the other information included below.

AREA CODES

The area code 02972 is for Junín de los Andes, 02944 is for Villa Traful, Villa la Angostura, Bariloche and El Bolsón, and 02945 is for Esquel and Trevelin.

Information booth in Bariloche.

WHEN TO GO

Apart from summer and Easter, the greatest tourist influx occurs in winter, when the ski centers open. Towns by lakes and rivers have more visitors during salmon fishing season.

USEFUL PHONE NUMBERS

- **Hospital Regional de Bariloche:** Tel. (02944) 42-6100.
- **Hospital El Bolsón:** Tel. (02944) 49-3681, 49-2838 y 49-3632.
- **Hospital Esquel:** Tel. (02945) 45-1074 y 45-1224.
- **Hospital Rural de Junín de los Andes:** Tel. (02945) 49-1162.
- **Hospital R.S. Castillo de San Martín de los Andes:** Tel. (02972) 42-7211.
- **Hospital Rural Dr. Oscar Arraiz de Villa La Angostura:** Tel. (02944) 49-4170.
- **Fire service:** Tel.100.
- **Police:** Tel.101.
- **Forest emergency:** Tel.105.
- **Local government:** Tel.106.
- **Hospital emergency:** Tel.107.

NATIONAL PARKS

- **Parque Nacional Lanín.** Headquarters: Emilio Frey 749, San Martín de los Andes. Tel. (02972) 42-7233.
- **Parque Nacional Nahuel Huapi.** Av. San Martín 211, San Carlos de Bariloche. Tel. (02944) 42 - 3111 / 42-3366.
- **Parque Nacional Arrayanes.** Puerto Quetrihué, w/n. Tel. (02944) 42 - 3111.
- **Parque Nacional Lago Puelo.** Lago Puelo, w/n. Tel. (02944) 49 - 9064.
- **Parque Nacional Los Alerces.** Ruta Provincial 71, w/n. Tel. (02945) 47 - 1015.

Parque Nacional Lanín Headquarters.

VISITING THE PARKS

Get information on park regulations and entrance rates from the national park headquarters and from the park warden's posts inside the parks. Special deals are available such as the Pase Verde (Green Pass), which entitles you to spend several days in Lanín park, Nahuel Huapi park and Lake Puelo.

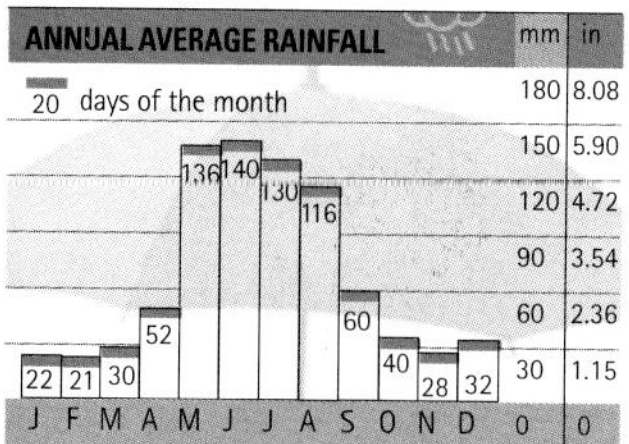

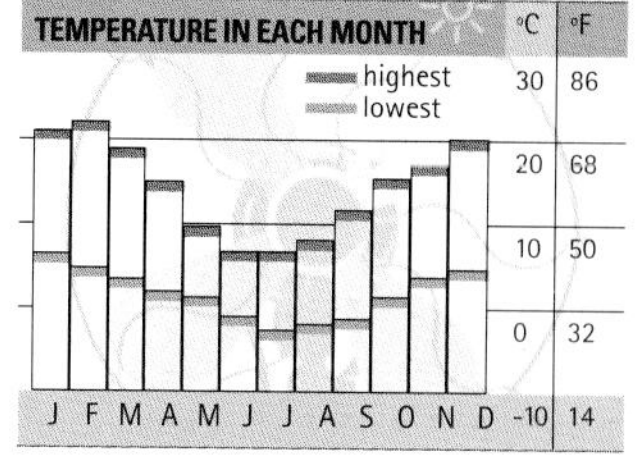

CLIMATE

The average temperature in Bariloche is 39°F in winter and 64°F in summer. Average annual rainfall is 800 mm.

SNOWY MONTHS

The heaviest snowfalls in the area are in June and September, when access to routes such as Siete Lagos may be closed. Visitors should bring warm clothing, sun cream and waterproof footwear.

Snowy woodland on Co. Chapelco.

FESTIVALS

Local festivals in the region include: the National Snow Festival (held at the ski centers), the Malt Festival in El Bolsón, the Community Festival, Indigenous Handicrafts Week in Junín de los Andes, Día del Montañes (Highland Day) and others.

9
JULIO
Independencia

MAIL

You can send or pick up letters, postcards and parcels at the mail office and at several local stores.

STORE SCHEDULES

Opening times for stores vary according to demand. However, in high season stores are usually open from 8 a.m. until nightfall.

TOURIST INFORMATION OFFICES

- **Junín de los Andes.** P. Milanesio and Cnel. Suárez. Tel. (02972) 49-1160.
- **San Martín de los Andes.** Rosas and Av. San Martín. Tel. (02972) 42-7695 / 42-6644.
- **Villa La Angostura.** Ruta de los Siete Lagos 96. Tel. (02944) 49-4124.
- **Bariloche.** 12 de Octubre 605 (Centro Cívico). Tel. (02944) 42-3188 and 42-3189.
- **El Bolsón.** San Martín and Roca. Tel. (02944) 49-2604.
- **Esquel.** Av. Alvear and Sarmiento. Tel. (02945) 45-1927.

WEATHER INFORMATION

Most hotels will provide you with weather forecasts, but you can also get meteoro-logical information from Tourist Information offices.

Sign in San Martín de los Andes.

0800-333-82667

State Tourism Department Information Center.

Call this toll-free number for tourist information on all the towns and regions in the country.

How to Travel

Just one means of transport is not enough to get around this region – Chair lifts, catamaran ferries, canoes and steam trains are tourist attractions in themselves, though for these southern roads what you need is a good off-road vehicle.

INFORMATION ON ROAD CONDITIONS

The region has a large network of roads; some are closed in winter due to snow, and others (i.e roads running through the parks) may be blocked by rock falls. For more information:

Junín de los Andes: Roads: Tel. (02972) 42 - 7403.
San Martín de los Andes: Provincial roads: Tel. (02972) 42 - 7403. National roads: (02972) 42 - 7410.
El Bolsón: roads: Tel. (02944) 49 -2527. Police: Tel. (02944) 49 - 2443.
Esquel: provincial roads: Tel. (02945) 45 - 1267.

CHEAPER GAS

South of the 42nd parallel, in El Bolsón, they sell gasoline at half price.

PASSES INTO CHILE

There are six border passes between Junín de los Andes, in Neuquén, and Trevelin, in Chubut. You'll need an ID card or a passport. Under 21's need permission.

CAR HIRE

- **AVIS**
  Tel. 0800-333-0101.
- **Dollar**
  Tel. (011) 4315-8800.
- **Hertz**
  Annie Millet
  Tel. (011) 4816-8001.

DEALING WITH SNOW

Anyone planning to travel Andean Patagonia by car, whatever the time of year, must be ready to deal with rough gravel, snow and ice on the roads. We recommend taking snow chains or special tires, as well as driving with great care. If your car goes into a skid on the gravel road, don't brake hard or spin the wheel – slow down using the accelerator.

BUS STATIONS

- **San Martín de los Andes:**
  General Villegas between Juez del Valle and Coronel Diaz.
  Tel. (02972) 42-7044.
- **Bariloche:**
  12 de Octubre 2400.
  Tel. (02944) 43-2860.
- **Esquel:**
  Av. Alvear and Fontana.
  Tel. (02945) 45-1566.

FACTS

INTERESTED IN HIRING A CAR?

All car rental companies in Bariloche have different plans for renting a car. The longer you hire it, the better value you will get. Ask forprices before arriving in the City.

THE CATANGO

This traditional oxcart is commonly used in the region.

NATIONAL PARKS

Some of the (often gravel) roads in the national parks may be difficult to use – for some you will need an off – road vehicle, while others may be closed in winter due to snow.

PARKING

No payment is necessary for parking in certain areas during the first 24 hours of your stay in some cities.

STEAM TRAINS

Some old steam trains have been brought back into circulation as a tourist attraction, such as the Old Patagonia Express (La Trochita) that runs between El Maitén and Esquel, and the Old Express which goes from Bariloche to Perito Moreno.

There are several airports in the region.

The Old Patagonia Express travels the steppes near Esquel.

AIRLINES

- **Aerolíneas Argentinas.** Tel. (02944) 42-3091 / 42-3161 / 42-2425.
- **LADE.** Tel. (02944) 42-3562.
- **LAPA/Dinar.** Tel. (02944) 43-7000 / 42-5500.
- **Southern Winds.** Tel. (02944) 42-3704.
- **Sapsa.** Tel. (02944) 43-2444 / 42-9012.

LAKE TRIPS

The main lakes in the region (Huechulafquen, Paimún, Lácar, Nahuel Huapi, Mascardí and Puelo) are all navigable, whether in individual boats or on organized trips in catamarans. Either options will get you to beaches, islands (Huemul and Victoria) and the Arrayanes forest.

Quay at Puerto Quetrihué.

AIRPORTS

Bariloche airport: (02944) 42-2555 / 6162; Chapelco airport, 24 km from San Martín de los Andes: (029 72) 42 - 8388; and Esquel airport: (02945) 45 - 1679.

Where to Sleep

The enormous lakes region offers a wide variety of accommodation options, all in harmony with nature. Choose from exclusive hotels and smaller hotels in beautiful settings, log cabins, lakeside camping areas and ski center complexes.

ITINERARY 1

HOTELS

Alejandro I ★★
RN 234 and Chubut, Junín de los Andes. Tel. (02972) 49-1182 / 49-1052.
Open for the sports fishing season, which usually takes place from November through April.

Hostería San Huberto ★★★
RP 60 km 33, río Malleo, Junín de los Andes. Tel. (02972) 49-1238.

CLOSER TO NATURE

Those who prefer an alternative form of accommodation which is closer to nature can choose from a wide range of campsites (including services or in the wild) in the lakes region. Or you can hire a wagon to sleep in!

Hostería Quillahué ★★★
RN 234, Jardines del Chimehuín quarter, Junín de los Andes. Tel. (02972) 49-1199 / 1419.
Very popular with fishermen from many different countries. Rooms decorated with fishing motifs.

Hostería Huechulafquen ★★
RP 61 km 55. Tel. (02972) 42-6075 / 7232.
At the foot of Lanín volcano, without telephone or television (they have a CB radio). Open from November through April.

Hostería El Montañés ★
San Martín 555, Junín de los Andes. Tel. (02972) 49-1155.

Refugio del Pescador ★
RP 61 km 57, lago Huechulafquen. Tel. (02972) 49-1319.
With nine-hole golf course, boat hire and walks.

Camping Las Toscas Blancas
At 1,500 m. point on RN 234.

Camping Santa Lucía
RP 61 km 7.

Camping Bahía Cañicul
RP 61 km 45.

Hotel San Jorge ★★
Lamadrid w/n, Junín de los Andes. Tel. (02972) 49-1147.

ITINERARY 2

HOTELS

Sol de los Andes ★★★★★
RP 19 w/n, San Martín de los Andes. Tel. (02972) 42-7460/8.

Le Chatelet ★★★★
Gral. Villegas 650, San Martín. Tel. (02972) 42-8294.

Las Balsas
Bahía Las Balsas, Villa La Angostura. Tel. (02944) 49-4308 / 4468.

FACTS

LAKESIDE STAYS

When you visit national parks such as Nahuel Huapi, you can stay in lakeside log cabins, hostels or luxury hotels on the shores of the main lakes: Nahuel Huapi, Espejo, Gutiérrez, Mascardi, Villarino, Huechulafquen and Lácar.

REFERENCES

NO CATEGORIZED	BAR
DOUBLE ROOM	SWIMMING POOL
TELEPHONE	LAUNDRY
TELEVISION	CAR PARK
AIR-CONDITIONING	TENTS
CENTRAL HEATING	HOT WATER
RESTAURANT	FIREPLACE

Hotel del Viejo Esquiador ★★★
Av. San Martín 1242, San Martín de los Andes. Tel. (02972) 42-7690 / 8283.

Le Village ★★★
Gral. Roca 816, San Martín de los Andes. Tel. (02972) 42-7698.

Chapelco Ski ★★
Belgrano 869, San Martín de los Andes. Tel. (02972) 42-7481.

Los Colonos del Sur ★
Rivadavia 686 , San Martín de los Andes. Tel. (02972) 42-7224.

Sol de los Andes ★★★
Cerro Comandante Díaz w/n, San Martín de los Andes. Tel. (02972) 42-7460 / 7468.

Torres del Sur ★★★
Coronel Díaz 1136, San Martín de los Andes. Tel. (02972) 42-5352.

Naum ★★
Coronel Díaz 1120, San Martín de los Andes. Tel. (02972) 42-8228.

HOTEL MESSIDOR

The presidents Arturo Frondizi and Isabel Perón both enjoyed the seclusion of this mansion, designed by Alejandro Bustillo in the style of a French castle.

Casa Grande Resort ★★★
Boulevard Quetrihué, Villa La Angostura. Tel. (02944) 49-4888.

Las Lomas del Correntoso ★★★
Ruta 231 and Lumilla, Villa La Angostura. Tel. (02944) 49-4484 / 4361.

La Cheminée ★★★
M. Moreno and Gral. Roca, San Martín de los Andes. Tel. (02972) 42-7617 / 7762.

Cabañas del Encuentro ★★
Capitán Drury 551, San Martín de los Andes. Tel. (02972) 42-9042 / 7197.

GUIDED TRIPS

A lot of hotels in Andean Patagonia offer guided trips and excursions, which include routes on horseback, mountain climbing, trips up mountains and even by hydroplane.

HOTELS

Panamericano ★★★★★
San Martín 532, Bariloche. Tel. (02944) 42-5846 / 50.

La Cascada ★★★★★
Av. Bustillo km 6, Circuito Chico. Tel. (02944) 44-1023 / 1088 / 1046.
An imposing building, designed by Bustillo. Originally constructed as the Cantilo family's summer residence. The Shah of Persia and the Queen of Denmark have stayed here.

Hotel El Casco ★★★★
Av. Bustillo km 11.6. Tel. (02944) 46-1032 / 1088.

Llao Llao ★★★★★
Av. Bustillo, km 26 , Circuito Chico. Tel. (02944) 44-8530.

MORE INFORMATION ON PAGE 80.

Amancay ★★★
Av. Bustillo km 24.8, Circuito Chico. Tel. (02944) 44-8344 / 8348.

Alaska Youth Hostel ★★
Lininque 31 (Av. Bustillo 7500), Bariloche. Tel. (02944) 46-1564.

Tivoli ★★
Mitre 382, Bariloche. Tel. (02944) 42-6155.

Aguas del Sur ★
Moreno 353, Bariloche. Tel. (02944) 42-2995.

Húngaro Gstaad ★★★
Av. Bustillo km 3,9, Circuito Chico. Tel. (02944) 44-1884.
Fully-equipped apartments available.

Le Petit Chalet ★★
Piedras and Francia, Bariloche. Tel. (02944) 42-3628.

Del Trébol ★
Av. Bustillo km 19, Circuito Chico. Tel. (02944) 44-8427.

Wonderland ★★★
Av. Bustillo 937, Bariloche. Tel. (02944) 42-5096.

Casita Suiza ★★
Quaglia 342, Bariloche. Tel. (02944) 42-3775.

Camping El Yeti
Av. Bustillo km 5.6, Circuito Chico. Tel. (02944) 44-2073.

Camping Petunia
Av. Bustillo km 13.5, Circuito Chico. Tel. (02944) 46-2196.

Le Bouquet ★★★
Av. Bustillo km 25, Circuito Chico. Tel. (02944) 44-8113.

Los Arcos ★★
Pioneros km 3.3, Bariloche. Tel. (02944) 44-1700.

Araucaria ★
Av. Bustillo km 8. Tel. (02944) 46-1502.

FOR FISHERMEN

All hotels catering for salmon fishing enthusiasts (on lakes such as Epuyen, Futalaufquen, Nahuel Huapi, Huechalafquen and others) are open from approximately November 15th through April 15th.

BADINO TURISMO

This firm organises tourist trips and activities (especially skiing) in Bariloche, Esquel, Villa La Angostura and San Martín de los Andes. Information: (02972) 42-7929 (San Martín de los Andes).

ITINERARY 4

HOTELS

Hotel Tronador ★★★
Lago Mascardi w/n. Tel. (02944) 44-1062.
Built in 1929 by the Vereertbrugghen family, this wooden building and its garden are situated between the mountain and a lake.

Club Hotel Catedral ★★★★
Villa Cerro Catedral w/n. Tel. (02944) 46-0006 / 0044.

Hotel Catedral Ski ★★★
Villa Cerro Catedral w/n. Tel. (02944) 46-0004 / 0007.

Daulaghiri ★★
Villa Cerro Catedral w/n. Tel. (02944) 46-0016.

Catedral Ski Village ★★
Villa Cerro Catedral w/n. Tel. (02944) 46-0037 / 0128.

Hostería Pire Hue ★★★★★
Villa Cerro Catedral w/n.
Tel. (02944) 46-0039 / 0040.

Alp Apart Hotel
Villa Cerro Catedral w/n.
Tel. (02944) 46-0105.

Departamentos del Cerro
Villa Cerro Catedral w/n.
Tel. (02944) 46-0026.

De Dinko
Villa Cerro Catedral w/n.
Tel. (02944) 46-0016.

El Retorno ★★★
Villa Los Coihues w/n, lago Gutiérrez.
Tel. (02944) 46-7333 / 7330.

Shekina ★★★
Villa Los Coihues w/n, lago Gutiérrez. Tel. (02944) 46-7422.

Hostería de la Villa ★★
Villa Cerro Catedral w/n.
Tel. (02944) 46-0071.

Hostería Landing ★★
Boock y Lanín (Melipal).
Tel. (02944) 44-1282.

Hostería del Gutiérrez ★
Ruta 253, lago Gutiérrez.
Tel. (02944) 46-7385.

Auto Camping W
Ruta 253, lago Gutiérrez.
Tel. (02944) 46-7332.

Camping Suizo
Ruta 253, lago Gutiérrez.
Tel. (02944) 46-7316.

Cabañas Palitos
Tronador 4150, Barrio de Melipal, Bariloche.
Tel. (02944) 44-2070.

HOTELS

La Casona de Odile ★★★
Barrio Luján km 6, El Bolsón.
Tel. (02944) 49-2753.
Log cabins for rent. With garden and trout farm.

Cordillera ★★★
San Martín 3210, El Bolsón.
Tel. (02944) 49-2235.

MOUNTAIN-STYLE

Many of the hotel complexes in this region include log cabin apartments with tiled gable roofs. Some of these include private parking space, a golf course, paddle tennis courts, swimming pools and even solariums.

AGROTOURISM

Some hotels (such as Cabaña Mico in El Bolsón) organise trips to small eco-friendly fruit-growing family farms. You are welcome to try the produce!

Hostería Los Notros
Salminiac 459, El Bolsón.
Tel. (02944) 49-2503.

Steiner
San Martín 600, El Bolsón.
Tel. (02944) 49-2224.

Hostería Enebros ★★
Ruta 16 w/n, camino al lago Puelo. Tel. (02944) 49-9054.

Hostería Olaf
Ruta 258, El Hoyo.
Tel. (02944) 47-1802.
With restaurant and Ahumamadero (which produces smoked meats and fish).

Esquel ★★
San Martín 1044, Esquel.
Tel. (02945) 45-2534.

Tehuelche ★★★
9 de Julio and Belgrano, Esquel.
Tel. (02945) 45-2420.

La Casona de Olgbrun
San Martín 1137, Esquel.
Tel. (02945) 45-3841 / 0536.

Los Notros
Sarmiento 425, Esquel.
Tel. (02945) 45-2218 / 4018.

La Tour d'Argent ★★
San Martín 1063, Esquel.
Tel. (02945) 45-4612 / 6450.

Cumbres Blancas ★★★
Ameghino 1683, Esquel.
Tel. (02945) 45-5100.

Where to Eat

This part of Andean Patagonia produces high quality fish, meat and game: trout, deer, wild boar and lamb are the cornerstones of local cuisine, which you can enjoy at an exclusive city restaurant or at an open-air barbecue stop. Smoked meats, mushrooms and chocolate add a distinctive flavour to the dishes.

ITINERARY 1

RESTAURANTS

La Tablita
Chile 206 and O´Higgins, Junín de los Andes. $

Huechulafquen
RP 61 km 51, lago Huechulafquen. Tel. (02972) 42-6075. $

Ruca Hueney
Padre Milanesio and Coronel Suárez, Junín de los Andes. Tel. (02972) 48-1113. $ $
Situated on a corner of Junín main square, this restaurant has a large main dining room and a menu featuring all kinds of meat and salmon.

Puerto Canoa
RP 61 km 52, lago Huechulafquen. Tel. (02972) 42-5065. $
Open-air barbecue tent by the quay (where you can take a catamaran trip round the lake).

Los Tres Hermanos
Padre Milanesio 330, Junín de los Andes. Tel. 49-1566. $

ITINERARY 2

RESTAURANTS

La Tasca
Mariano Moreno 866, San Martín de los Andes. $
Tel. (02972) 42-8663 / 7314.

Mendieta
Av. San Martín 713, San Martín de los Andes. Tel. (02972) 42-9301. $

Pioneri
Gral. Roca and Sarmiento, San Martín de los Andes. Tel. (02944) 42-5640. $
Specialities include salmon carpaccio and trout au gratin (with local cheeses).

Avataras
Teniente Ramayón 765, San Martín de los Andes. Tel. (02972) 42-7104. $ $
A restaurant with a menu comprised of top-class regional and international cuisine including a number of Japanese dishes.

La Terraza
Ruta 65 km 35.5, Villa Traful. Tel. (02944) 47-9077. $ $
You must try the selection of local dried meats, and the rose ice cream.

Confitería Pradera del Puma
Centro de esquí Chapelco s/n, San Martín de los Andes. $

Naranjo en Flor
Chucao 62, Puerto Manzano, Villa La Angostura. Tel. (02944) 49-4863. $ $
The curried lamb, pork in pine-nut sauce and the tapas (snacks) are particularly tasty.

FINE IMPORTS

Some of the best restaurants in San Martín de los Andes offer a number of exclusive imported goods, such as these Havana cigars, imported from Cuba by Avataras.

PRICE RANGE

Ⓢ Inexpensive

Ⓢ Ⓢ Medium-priced

Ⓢ Ⓢ Ⓢ Expensive

Both restaurants and bars exhibit prices on the menu on the window-shop or outside the premises.

TASTY WOODLAND FLAVOURS

The most commonlyused mushrooms in Patagonian cuisine are the ones that grow on pines (holletus) and the ones from cypresses and morels (Morchela esculeita). They go well with meat, sauces, pasta and fish.

RESTAURANTS

Ahumadero Weiss
Vicealmirante O'Connor 401, Bariloche.
Tel. (02944) 43-5789. Ⓢ
Wide range of smoked fish and meats and cheeses.

Casita Suiza
Quaglia 342, Bariloche. Ⓢ Ⓢ
Tel. (02944) 42-3775 / 42-6111.

La Marmite
Mitre 329, Bariloche.
Tel. (02944) 42-3685. Ⓢ Ⓢ

Cervecería Blest
Av. Bustillo km 11.6, Circuito Chico. Tel. (02944) 46-1026. Ⓢ
Includes specialities from Central European cuisine.
MORE INFORMATION ON PAGE 81.

Chez Philippe
Primera Junta 980, Bariloche.
Tel. (02944) 42-7291. Ⓢ Ⓢ

Chalet Suisse
San Martín 630, Bariloche.
Tel. (02944) 42-3120. Ⓢ

El Boliche de Alberto
Av. Bustillo km 8.8, Circuito Chico. Tel. (02944) 46-2285. Ⓢ

CHOCOLATE

Bariloche chocolate is delicious when eaten on its own, mixed with fruit or in the form that has made it famous – in sticks.

El Patacón
Av. Bustillo km 7, Circuito Chico.
Tel. (02944) 44-2898. Ⓢ Ⓢ
Former President Clinton, enjoyed the meat dishes here.

Curantos Emilio Goye
Félix Goye w/n, Colonia Suiza.
Tel. (02944) 42-8976. Ⓢ

RESTAURANTS

Rodeo
Villa Cerro Catedral w/n.
Tel. (02944) 46-0001. Ⓢ

Ski Ranch
Villa Cerro Catedral w/n.
Tel. (02944) 46-0116. Ⓢ
Try the goulash, the Patagonian lamb, the Locro stew or the trout.

Punta Nevada
Villa Cerro Catedral w/n.
Tel. (02944) 46-0134. Ⓢ Ⓢ

El Refugio
Villa Cerro Catedral w/n.
Tel. (02944) 46-0124. Ⓢ

ITINERARY 5

RESTAURANTS

La Casona de Odile
Barrio Luján km 6, El Bolsón.
Tel. (02944) 49-2753. Ⓢ
Farm with trout farm. Can serve a maximum of 12 diners.

Arcimboldo
Sarmiento 1617, El Bolsón.
Tel. (02944) 49-2137. Ⓢ

Jauja
Av. San Martín 2867, El Bolsón.
Tel. (02944) 49-2448. Ⓢ

Cassis
Sarmiento 1200, Esquel.
Tel. (02945) 45-0576. Ⓢ Ⓢ

La Tour d'Argent
San Martín 1063, Esquel.
Tel. (02945) 45-4612. Ⓢ

Where to Have Fun

One of the region's greatest attractions is its excellent winter sports infrastructure, which includes some of South America's largest ski centers. However, apart from skiing, visitors can enjoy a wide range of leisure activities to suit all tastes.

SKI CENTERS

The itineraries in this guidebook include five winter sports centers – but there is another one: Caviahue ski center, near Neuquén.

Chapelco
Av. San Martín and Elordi (San Martín de los Andes).
Tel. (02972) 42-7845.
www.chapelco.com.ar

Cerro Bayo
RP 66 km 6, Villa La Angostura.
Tel. (02944) 49-4189.

Catedral Alta Patagonia
Villa Cerro Catedral w/n.
Tel. (02944) 42-3776.
www.altapatagonia.com.ar

Centro de Recreo Invernal Piedras Blancas (Cerro Otto)
Av. Bustillo km 5, Bariloche.
Tel. (02944) 42-8811.

Cerro Perito Moreno
Ruta 258 km 4, El Bolsón.
Tel. (02944) 49-3912.

Centro de Actividades de Montaña La Hoya
Info.: tel. (02945) 45-2420.

Fireworks at Cerro Catedral.

THE SNOW FESTIVAL

In August, the National Snow Festival is held at Cerro Catedral winter sports center, with fireworks and a torchlight procession of skiers skiing down to base camp. This festival is also held at other centers.

HIGH AND LOW SEASONS

Visitors pay different rates for snow sports according to the time of year. The year is divided into low season, midseason (30% higher rates) and high season.

COMPETITIONS

Most of the winter sports competitions in the area are held in August, while at Catedral, Chapelco and other centers, international championships are held for slope skiing, alpine skiing, cross-country skiing and snowboarding. There are also exhibitions of "ski-dressage".

Classes

Teaching winter sports is an important feature at the ski centers. Classes are available with experienced teachers – including ski instructors brought in from Europe in low season. There are group classes for all ages and levels.

FACTS

GOING UP
Apart from the chair ski lifts there are also drag lifts: place your skis parallel, relax your body and raise your sticks off the ground.

2,500 SETS OF SKI EQUIPMENT FOR HIRE AT CATEDRAL ALTA PATAGONIA

Services

Mountain refuges with VIP lounges, cyber cafes, bars, cafes, terrace bars, tearooms, restaurants and accommodation – you can find all these at the ski centers; wooden, alpine-style constructions that harmonize beautifully with the landscape.

Skiers at Cerro Chapelco.

BETTER PRICES
There are reduced rates for young people, as well as family discounts on one-week passes, equipment hire, ski classes and kindergartens for small children.

Chair lift at a ski center.

Skiing goggles.

Snowboard.

Ski sticks.

Equipment

Skis, boots, bindings and sticks (plus the accessories) are all indispensable items, and should be selected according to each person's level of skiing ability. Hire them at the ski centers or in specialist stores.

Skiing jacket.

Boots.

Skis.

TO MOTOR
Those who want high-speed snow travel with a little less physical effort can rent snowmobiles at the ski centers.

Snowmobile at Cerro Chapelco.

DOG SLEDS. Dog-sledging with teams of Siberian Huskies is one of the new snow sports available.

Dog sledging.

Adventure Sports

Fun in the Andes is not just limited to winter – all year you can go mountain biking, canoeing, rafting, off-road driving, trekking, climbing, horse-riding and kayaking and many other activities in the beautiful great outdoors.

River Malleo is one of the most popular rivers for rafting.

Rafting

There are several levels of difficulty: from the beginner to the more daring rafter. The Limay River is a gentle river with beautiful landscape, while the lower Manso river has rapids with different levels of difficulty. Take comfortable clothing – and a change of clothing for afterwards!

PARAGLIDING

Paragliding from the Otto, Catedral or Piltriquitrón mountains gives you an amazing view of the landscape. Try a two-person paraglider (with an instructor). The flight lasts around 20 minutes.

WATER SPORTS

Playa Bonita and Bahía Serena are just two spots which are ideal for jet skis and windsurfing, in the strong summer breezes.

OFF-ROAD CIRCUITS

Several companies offer organized trips in off-road vehicles that can get along routes that are inaccessible to other types of cars. Take one of these trips, and drive off along quiet, traffic-free roads to lookout points with fantastic views.

HORSE RIDING

There are all kinds of rides available – for families as well as for experienced riders. They range from one-day to seven-day circular routes, always with a guide and usually with meals included.

Mountain Biking

Use your own bicycle or a rented one to explore the many cycle paths in this region, though always take a guide and suitable equipment. The most popular biking areas are Bariloche, the Mt. Tronador area, the Catedral and Chapelco mountains and Lake Gutiérrez.

ARCHERY is another option. Archery competitions are held in Chapelco.

Trekking

Routes available for all ages. Clothing and footwear should be comfortable and hard-wearing, and trekkers can spend the night in shelters during longer walks. Always take a guide and follow the regulations for each national Park. Mountaineering clubs provide reliable information.

Beautiful waterfalls and great lookout points.

WATERFALLS, *Streams, lookout points, mountain refuges and forests packed with flora and fauna are just some of the attractions of trekking. Choose from easier, flat routes or steeper, more difficult ones.*

Trekkers with a park warden.

Forest ramblers.

GAME HUNTING

Red deer and wild boar are highly-prized by hunters. Big and small game hunting is permitted in certain areas. Hunters should be at least 18, use authorized arms and have a permit.

Statue of deer.

CLIMBING

Bariloche Mountaineering Club will provide you with information on the best spots for experienced climbers. Cerro Otto is a very popular climbing spot.

Where to Shop

Apart from outdoor and leisure activities, the Andean Patagonia corridor is also great for shopping. You can't visit the South without checking out the craft fairs filled with pieces made from ceramics, fabrics, leather, wood, wool and silver, all in a mixture of European and Indian styles.

Shopping

The big cities of Andean Patagonia combine a wide selection of shops and department stores with the preservation of traditional crafts: one of the areas in Argentina where tradition and infrastructure are perfectly interwoven.

GAUCHO in hand-painted ceramics.
▮ **Casa de Muñecas**
Av. Bustillo, km 23.4, Circuito Chico.

KITCHEN UTENSILS
A wooden cooking bowl and spoon carved in the Indian style are available at crafts fairs.

HOMEMADE

Much of the handcrafted tradition is influenced by the first European colonies, Indian traditions and the young people who came to places such as El Bolsón in the 1960s. The result is pieces made of wood, ceramics, iron, leather and local fabrics.

MAPUCHE DESIGNS
Mapuche craft traditions are visible in the geometric designs on present-day fabrics and leather goods.
▮ *Padre Milanesio 568, Junín.*

PITCHERS
Small wooden vessel with handle, from Junín de los Andes.

LEATHER AND METAL
Knife with tooled handle and sheath made from an animal's hoof.

SWEATERS
Mountain-style woolen sweaters and waistcoats.

SILVER
"Three-story" necklaces and metal rings originally came from the Mapuche.

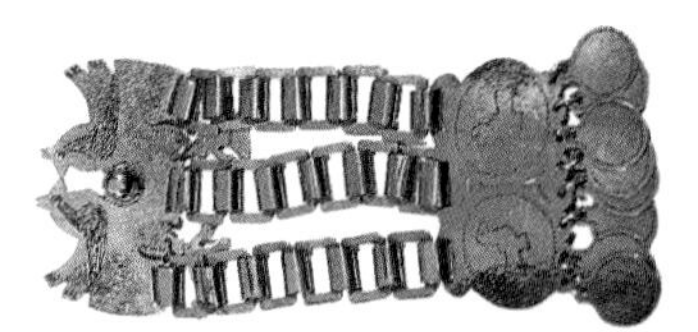

HAND-PAINTED AND ENAMELED
Decorated tea sets made "Bariloche Ceramics" famous.

TRADITIONAL BEER
The availability of malt in El Bolsón led to beer being brewed without chemical additives.

CERAMICS
The Bariloche ceramics company was created in 1948 by Luís Razza. They produce enameled and hand-painted majolica pieces with floral, European and Indian motifs.
Mitre 112, Bariloche.

FAIRYTALE HOUSE
La Casa de Muñecas (Doll's house) – right on the Circuito Chico – sells these ceramic mountain-style houses.

WOODLAND SPIRITS
Spirits and magical creatures from the imaginary world of local tales and legends.
Moreno and Villegas, Bariloche.

PAINTED ROOSTER
This figure has been modeled, painted and enameled by hand, using methods of European origin.

LOCAL FAIRS

The most famous of these is the weekly fair at El Bolsón, though craft fairs are also held in Bariloche, San Martín de los Andes and Junín de los Andes, among others.

DRUM
Indian wind and percussion instruments, used in ceremonies. **Paseo Artesanal.** *Padre Milanesio 568, Junín de los Andes.*

ACKNOWLEDGEMENTS

Ahumadero Weiss
Aldo Vilosio
Armando de Giacomo
Fernando Galíndez, Architect
González de Estrada, Architect
Guillermo Frontera, Architect
Liliana Lolich, Architect
Cabaña Micó
Cabañas de Ovejas Belvedere
Casa Thumann
Centro de Deportes Invernales Catedral Alta Patagonia
Centro de Deportes Invernales Chapelco
Chocolates Abuela Goye
Claudia Tavares
Daniel Beltrame
Daniel Marandet
Daniel Marchetti
Diego Fernández
Dirección Municipal de Turismo de Junín de los Andes
Eve Bignolo
Fernando Sánchez
Fundación Vida Silvestre
Gabriela Pastor
Hotel Llao Llao
Iglesia de Nuestra Señora de las Nieves (Junín de los Andes)
Iglesia de Nuestra Señora de Nahuel Huapi (San Carlos de Bariloche)
Intendencia del Parque Nacional Arrayanes
Intendencia del Parque Nacional Lago Puelo
Intendencia del Parque Nacional Lanín
Intendencia del Parque Nacional Los Alerces
Intendencia del Parque Nacional Nahuel Huapi
Javier Alvarez Lamas
Laura Barrientos
Leonardo Gasset
Magdalena García
Mauro Guevara
Michelle Eyerhabide
Mónica Kapusta (Press Officer to the Secretaría de Turismo y Deporte)
Museo Galés de Trevelín
Omar Contreras
Raúl Ovalle
Rubén Neyra (Head Warden at Parque Nacional Los Alerces)
Secretaría de Turismo de Chubut
Secretaría de Turismo de Esquel
Secretaría de Turismo de la provincia del Neuquén
Secretaría de Turismo de la provincia de Río Negro
Secretaría de Turismo de San Carlos de Bariloche
Secretaría de Turismo de San Martín de los Andes
Secretaría de Turismo de Trevelín
Secretaría de Turismo de Villa La Angostura
Silvio Fuentes
Sonia Miriam Soto Arcos
Stella Maris Sano
Teresita Peláez
Víctor Arrechea